ROUTLEDGE LIBRARY EDITIONS:
TELEVISION

Volume 14

THE FUTURE OF BROADCASTING

THE FUTURE OF BROADCASTING

A Report presented to The Social Morality Council, October 1973

SOCIAL MORALITY COUNCIL

Routledge
Taylor & Francis Group
LONDON AND NEW YORK

First published in 1974

This edition first published in 2013
by Routledge
2 Park Square, Milton Park, Abingdon, Oxon, OX14 4RN

Simultaneously published in the USA and Canada
by Routledge
711 Third Avenue, New York, NY 10017

Routledge is an imprint of the Taylor & Francis Group, an informa business

First issued in paperback 2016

British Library Cataloguing in Publication Data
A catalogue record for this book is available from the British Library

ISBN: 978-0-415-83994-5 (hbk)

ISBN: 978-0-415-83994-5 (pbk)

Publisher's Note
The publisher has gone to great lengths to ensure the quality of this reprint but points out that some imperfections in the original copies may be apparent.

Disclaimer
The publisher has made every effort to trace copyright holders and would welcome correspondence from those they have been unable to trace.

THE FUTURE OF BROADCASTING

A Report presented to
The Social Morality Council

October 1973

EYRE METHUEN
LONDON

First published 1974

Printed in Great Britain for
Eyre Methuen Ltd
11 New Fetter Lane, London EC4P 4EE
by Butler & Tanner Ltd
Frome and London

ISBN 0 413 31140 6

MEMBERS OF THE COMMISSION

Dame Margaret Miles (Chairman)
Dame Elizabeth Ackroyd
Agneilus Andrew, O.F.M.
Catherine Avent
Dr Jay G. Blumler
Dr Jeremy Bray
The Rt Hon. Lord Brown
Dame Anne Bryans
Sir Ronald Gould
Alan Hill, C.B.E.
The Rev. Douglas Hubery
Dipak Nandy
Joslyn G. Owen
Stella Richman
Jean Rowntree
John Scupham
Jack Straw
The Rt Rev. Oliver Tomkins
Oliver Whitley
John Harriott, S.J. (Rapporteur)
Janet M. Mortimer (Secretary)

Observers

Ian Alexander	*Foreign and Commonwealth Office*
L. J. Burrows, O.B.E.	*Department of Education and Science*
Col. Robert Hornby, O.B.E.	
Dennis Lawrence, O.B.E.	*Ministry of Posts and Telecommunications*
Edward Oliver	*Secretary General, Social Morality Council*

Members of the Commission took part in their individual capacities and not as representatives of organisations.

The Social Morality Council was founded in 1969 to foster mutual understanding between religious believers and non-believers, and to undertake joint studies of major social issues in the light of ethical values.

Address: 17 York House
London W8 4EY

CONTENTS

INTRODUCTION

This Report, commissioned by the Social Morality Council* in 1972, is offered as a modest contribution to public debate on the future of broadcasting. The SMC initiative was taken at that time partly because the Charter of the BBC and the Act which established the IBA were thought to be due for renewal and revision in 1976. The Government has since postponed the date to 1981, but this decision does not diminish the need for informed public debate; indeed, though the Government still does not intend to set up a full-scale inquiry, the Minister of Posts and Telecommunications has invited opinions and suggestions on such questions as the use of the Fourth Channel and regional broadcasting needs. The postponed date has in fact increased the opportunity for constructive debate.

Our Report has no official blessing or sponsorship, and has no pretensions to be a substitute for the sort of wide-ranging inquiry the Government has commissioned in the past; it is merely an attempt by a few interested lay people to make a socially and morally responsible examination of some of the important questions which issue from broadcasting (particularly television). As might be

*The Social Morality Council brings together humanists and religious believers of various faiths to search for common ground and undertake joint studies of contemporary social issues.

expected, we did not always agree about everything but on many basic issues there was a remarkable consensus.

Time and resources have been limited, but what we had were used well. In the course of our meetings over a period of nine months we heard evidence from, and had full and interesting discussions with, many experts in the field of broadcasting.

The members of the Commission were invited to serve as private individuals and not as representatives of organisations. Every attempt was made to embrace differing views and varied professional expertise. Such balance was not easy to achieve (after all, everyone is involved to some extent in broadcasting) and it changed according to the pattern of acceptance and the ability of members to attend meetings. The group as finally constituted included some people who had worked voluntarily or professionally in broadcasting, others who had no direct experience except as viewers and listeners. No member was currently directly involved in either of the broadcasting organisations or in Government.

We hope that the Report will be widely read; it therefore includes a considerable amount of information which will be familiar to people within the industry, but which to many of us was new and of absorbing interest.

The experience of trying to take an overall view of such an enormous field has been daunting but stimulating and exciting. Although we deliberately excluded a number of issues – external services, religious broadcasting, which is being dealt with fully by the Church of England Report, conditions of employment, which is included in the Report prepared by the ACTT – we have been constantly aware of the impossibility of covering the ground or of doing justice to our subject with the limited resources at our disposal.

We have received most generous cooperation from the BBC and the IBA, and are most grateful to those many people who have met us and talked with us in so frank and friendly a way. We have also had most helpful assistance from the Ministry of Posts and Telecommunications.

Our Report is in no sense revolutionary, but neither is it a complacent defence of the *status quo*. We have tried to look at the present pattern of broadcasting, its strengths and its weaknesses, and to discover where change is needed. Then, in the light of rapid technological and social change, and conscious of the need to preserve the traditions of independence and democracy which have characterised British broadcasting, we have tried to make some suggestions about the possible directions of change.

As Chairman, I should like to thank most warmly all the members of the Commission, and several observers who attended regularly, for their generous support and for attending long meetings at the end of a day's work. Finally, the thanks of all of us are due to our rapporteur, John Harriott, and the secretary, Janet Mortimer, for incredible feats of drafting and minuting.

We believe that the SMC has performed a useful service in commissioning this inquiry and we commend it to everyone interested in the future of the broadcasting services.

Dame Margaret Miles, D.B.E.
(*Chairman*)

1 THE GOALS OF BROADCASTING

I believe television is going to be the test of the modern world, and that in this new opportunity to see beyond the range of our vision we shall discover either a new and unbearable disturbance of the general peace or a saving radiance in the sky. We shall stand or fall by television – of that I am quite sure.

E. B. WHITE, 1938

The British Broadcasting Company, from 1926 the British Broadcasting Corporation, was inaugurated in 1922 and has provided domestic radio services ever since. In 1932 it began its overseas transmissions. In 1936 the television service was begun, and after closing down during the Second World War, re-opened in 1946. In 1954 the Independent Television Authority was set up by Act of Parliament to operate an alternative television service, and under its new title of Independent Broadcasting Authority will, from the autumn of 1973, oversee all commercial radio broadcasting. Within fifty years the hobby of a few private enthusiasts has grown into a vast industry and broadcasting become a pervasive factor in the life of the entire population. It seems an appropriate time to ask whether, in the light of social changes and new technical developments, the broadcasting services as we know them are pursuing the best possible goals and meeting whatever needs it is in their nature to satisfy; or whether radical changes or substantial adjustments are called for.

Television-viewing is far and away the most popular pastime in the country. Nearly half the population (Opinion Research Centre Survey, 1968) devotes most of its leisure time to viewing. Any evening of the week over seven million people will watch television and on special occasions, like the *Eurovision Song Contest*, the figure may rise to over twenty-five million (BBC Audience Research). The average time spent viewing is nineteen hours a week (BBC/IBA figure). The audience is roughly divided fifty-fifty between the BBC's two channels and the IBA's one. 95 per cent of all British households possess television and 20 per cent colour television, a figure which is rising.

In 1971/2 BBC 1 transmitted 4,417 hours of television, 3,671 of them in colour. BBC 2 transmitted 2,545 hours, 2,083 of them in colour. Including all regional variations, the Independent Television system as a whole provided 7,900 hours of television. In the same year the BBC provided 23,871 hours of radio transmission on its four national networks. To these figures must be added the output of the BBC's twenty local radio stations and, before long, that of the eighteen commercial radio stations which IBA expect to have in operation by the summer of 1976; and in five towns – Bristol, Greenwich, Sheffield, Swindon and Wellingborough – the Ministry of Posts and Telecommunications is supervising experiments in local cable television.

Not only is the sheer volume of television and radio output impressive, so too is its variety of subject matter. In theory, on *one* day chosen at random and allowing for regional variations, the listener/viewer could tune to programmes on: the private life of the herring gull, oil-painting, diplomacy, a nostalgic walk through the countryside, the history of Turkey, the US Senate's Un-American Activities Committee, Scottish dancing, people frightened of flying, and the painter Géricault, in addition to the usual ration of serials, feature films, educational programmes, light entertainment, plays, news and sport. In theory only, for in actual practice most people can only watch television or listen to the radio at certain periods of the day, a fact which will have some importance in later sections of this Report.

If the sheer volume, ubiquity and variety of broadcasting production is impressive so also is its cost. In 1971/2 BBC expenditure on domestic services, financed out of the licence fee, amounted to £112,424,000 and the cost of commercial services to approximately £100,000,000. One hour of television costs on average £7,000 and one hour of radio £934, but the most expensive items, such as an opera, a light entertainment spectacular, or an episode of a film series like *The Persuaders*, may cost as much as £100,000. In 1970 a *Play for Today* cost the BBC about £25,000, an episode of *Dad's Army* about £15,000 and a sports programme such as *Grandstand* about £4,000 an hour;* inflation and rising cost would of course

*Brian Groombridge, *Television and the People* (Penguin), p. 16; and *In the Public Interest* (BBC).

increase these figures considerably today. It is estimated that the capital costs of activating a fourth television channel would be in the region of £30 m. and the annual running costs, depending on the kind of service provided, between £15 m. and £30 m. Yet the costs of the broadcasting services as such are less than half of the total volume of money spent by the public on the means of reception – radio and television sets and the like.

In addition to their economic cost, the broadcasting services also make heavy demands on a national resource – airspace – which can be measured quantitively in terms of Hertz and MegaHertz. This point has been made dramatically by Brian Groombridge:*

> To send a telegram, a communications channel occupies only 200 Hz; a telephone circuit requires 3,000 Hz; but to send out a high quality television picture with sound takes up 8 million Hz (8 MHz). There is only one spectrum with a physical limit to the range of suitable frequencies. A society which invests in one television channel transmitting sound and vision in one direction, may have to do without a thousand two-way telephones or 40,000 teleprinters. Just as earth and water have to be conserved and their uses properly considered, so do radio waves.

Employees of the two broadcasting institutions number tens of thousands. In addition, the prosperity of a vast army of people ranging from those working in the manufacturing industry to freelance contributors depends on the existence of broadcasting services. Both the broadcasting institutions make intensive use of Post Office facilities and services. In short, the programmes which the public sees and hears are only the most visible part of an enormous industry with ramifications in many areas of national life.

Broadcasting therefore represents a huge financial, technical and social investment. In return it supplies a variety of social needs. Like Parliament, the Law, the Church, and the Press, the broadcasting system is now woven into the social fabric of the nation and, some would argue, exercises as much, if not more, influence upon people's lives as any of these, though the necessarily painstaking task of collecting evidence to determine the exact nature of this influence is still far from complete.

This impressionistic description of the broadcasting services as they exist leads on to another consideration: their character. The

*Op. cit., p. 16.

character of British broadcasting has largely been determined by the social context in which it first developed, and the dominating personality of the BBC's first Director General, John Reith. From the beginning, broadcasting was envisaged as a public service with the good of the individual and society as its paramount concern. Even when the advent of commercial television broke the monopoly enjoyed by the BBC – a public corporation established by Royal Charter – this notion of public service was defined by Act of Parliament as the first duty of the new authority, and various conditions were written into the Act to curb the use of broadcasting for commercial advantage. The concept that broadcasting must be the servant of the public still underpins all the broadcasting services in Britain, although the interpretation of this formula has undergone modification over the years. For this, not only commercial pressures but theories about society, and actual changes in the make-up of society, are responsible. In the words of Howard Newby of the BBC: 'Broadcasting is not a matter of providing basic products for an unchanging public. Society changes, tastes alter, fashion dictates, and all in a way that no one quite understands, far less controls.' The introduction of a network devoted to pop music, or the change from a policy of mixed programming to one providing four networks, each of a markedly different character, are examples of attempts by the BBC to accommodate shifts in public taste and social habits. But different concepts of public service can go deeper. Sir John Reith viewed society as a hierarchy, a pyramid, and believed that the task of the broadcasting services was gradually to familiarise those at the bottom with the high culture and values of an élite at the top. For this, the 'brute force of monopoly' was the necessary effective instrument. By the 1960s, when the BBC monopoly had been broken and society bore a more egalitarian stamp, Reith's view gave way to Sir Hugh Greene's that the broadcasting services should be a kind of market-place in which all kinds of dissentient voices could be heard. Now, although it is still scarcely more than a faint shift in the wind, the growing enthusiasm for access and participation in all areas of life is putting pressure on the broadcasting institutions to place the means of communication in the hands of those who feel they have something to say instead of reserving them for those who are professionally trained or officially invited to broadcast: in short, to break down the barrier between the élite who transmit and the mass who listen and view. It is probably a mistake to think of each of these theories of broadcasting as exclusive of the others. Each has some validity, all complement each other, and room must be found for all of them in a thorough-going service of broadcasting.

Before considering what a broadcasting service can reasonably be expected to do, it is necessary to evaluate the importance of communications within society as a whole, the nature and values of that society, and the characteristics of broadcasting precisely as a medium of communication.

Whether British society was ever dominated by a single creed and code of behaviour is highly debatable. Today, undoubtedly, it is a pluralist society – criss-crossed by a variety of cultures and sub-cultures, value systems, customs, habits, moral codes, religions and ideologies. Recent successive waves of immigration have meant that many British citizens do not share the common Christian inheritance. It is also a society in which ideas, enthusiasms and fashions change rapidly. In his book, *The New Anatomy of Britain*,* Anthony Sampson says, for example: 'At the beginning of the sixties such words as environment, consumers, ecology, participation, permissiveness, feedback . . . were hardly muttered in polite society. Now the environment has its own department, everyone is a consumer, and participation is the small change of politicians' weekend speeches.' And like most industrialised societies it is increasingly urban, mobile and politically, socially and technologically complex. In such a diversified society, even though it may contain a larger residue of traditional values than is sometimes supposed, it is not easy for broadcasting to support a particular hierarchy of values or to be a focus of definite cultural, religious and ethical values. At one and the same time it has a part in determining the kind of society that exists and is itself determined by the kind of society that exists.

Another feature of modern society is its dependence on systems of rapid communication. A battery of instruments of communication – books, letters, newspapers, radio, telegraph, telephone, television, telex, etc. – is to hand, while technological advances are continually adding to their number. Among these instruments radio and television are of outstanding value and importance, but the fact is sometimes overlooked that their importance is relative, and that other instruments can perform certain tasks that they cannot, or perform them better. To decide how much of the nation's wealth is to be spent on this or that system of communications as a social desideratum involves difficult social and political judgements. Is it, for example, if money is limited, more important to improve the telephone service

*(Hodder and Stoughton), p. xvi.

or to provide a new television network? Or are both such vital necessities that society must be willing to forgo other social services so that both can be provided? Is the provision of communications systems more or less important to a modern society than the supply of roads, schools, hospitals and other social services, and are some forms of communication so important to society that they deserve Government subsidy even though they cannot pay their way? Such questions are not yet sufficiently familiar to admit definite answers. But the answers have a bearing on the future provision of broadcasting services.

Broadcasting is one medium of communication among many: it is distinct from, say, the telephone or the daily newspaper. Each particular medium has its own peculiar characteristics, and if, in the case of broadcasting, these are ignored, it is possible that the public will expect from its broadcasting services something which it is not in their power to provide. What then are the strengths and weaknesses of radio and television as such? As to their strengths, both can be used to communicate with a small localised or a mass audience; both can communicate to their audience a common experience, and disseminate ideas, information and entertainment with immediacy and considerable dramatic force; both can range widely – even across national frontiers – carrying messages from far afield to the intimacy of the home. Both can be used for multiple purposes to provide theatre, news services, documentaries, sport, discussion, music, etc. Both can be used in conjunction with other media – telephone, films, booklets, records – to increase their effectiveness. Radio has demonstrated an exceptional capacity to stimulate the imagination, and television to bring home realities which for many people are beyond imagining. As to the weaknesses, there is the fact that airspace is rationed and only a limited number of channels or networks can be made available. Cable transmission will eventually multiply the possible sources of broadcasting but probably not with comprehensive coverage of the country within the next decade, and even then such sources will not be infinite. Any one service or channel has only so much available airtime with competing claims upon it. Broadcasting is uniform: within a given transmission area or group of transmission areas linked for the purpose, on a particular channel the same programme, and only that programme, is receivable everywhere. Both radio and television, the latter especially, virtually demand full attention except when music is used purely as a background noise. Both are exclusive: no matter how many services are receivable, viewers and listeners can only use one at a time.

Neither possesses a captive audience nor can guarantee to attract and hold all the people it attempts to reach, nor can be certain that the messages sent out are clearly understood, or that the use made of them is the use intended by the senders. Neither can be stopped in its tracks to be digested at leisure, questioned or criticised (except rather clumsily through the phone-in or studio audience); neither (leaving out of account videotape and sound cassettes) can be re-run until its matter has been mastered. The need to process and edit material imposes an intermediary between event and audience, and in so doing may impose value judgements as well. Both communicate only what can be seen and heard, and only so much of these, and, by highlighting certain details of some area of life, may in fact give a false picture of the whole. Both require technical facilities, equipment, resources and professional skills which limit their use to those who have acquired at least some minimal training, and finally, both radio and television are constrained by the human limitations in wisdom, knowledge, ingenuity, professional competence, artistry, imagination, industry, honesty and ideas of those who control and use them. In a phrase, television and radio are uniquely the media of mass communication, but not all that is worth communicating can be communicated to the mass, or be best communicated through the mass media.

The audience for radio and television comprises virtually the whole of the British public, the whole age-range, the complete social and educational spectrum – all sorts and conditions of men. Each individual within this audience possesses his own set of tastes, interests, aspirations and opinions, each his variety of moods. Yet media of mass communication – television more than radio – because they are capable of addressing huge and differentiated audiences, tend to restrict the variety of subject matter they deal with, and the transience of their messages, together with shortage of space and time, operate against depth of treatment. These tendencies stem naturally from the characteristics of the medium. They are the defects of their virtues; and both defects and virtues are inherent. They do not derive from forms of organisation or methods of finance, though the forms and methods might be such as to reinforce or guard against one or the other. Secondly, viewers and listeners have only a limited time to watch and listen, and cannot attend to more than one programme at a time, though criticisms of the broadcasting services often ignore this simple fact. If the services are judged as a whole, there are probably far more programmes that the average viewer would choose to watch than he has the opportunity to watch. Thirdly, there is no saying how any particular programme will touch the taste or mood of a particular person at a particular moment. In a recent book, McQuail, Blumler and Brown state categorically: 'There is no ... correspondence between the place on the presumed scale of cultural worth to which programme material may be assigned ... and the depth of meanings that may be drawn from them by many of their most keen attenders.'* Different individuals may use the same programme material as a means of serious instruction, an imaginative way of working out personal problems, a relief from boredom, or a stimulus to working more rapidly and cheerfully.† Fourthly, a particular subject may be of more or less importance to an individual according to circumstances; even the most serious-minded person may, at certain times, be more concerned about an idea for a new recipe than proofs of the existence of God.

One conclusion that may be drawn from the multiplicity and variability of viewer needs, interests and responses, tells against the principle of audience maximisation – that of finding out which programme items get the biggest audiences and then providing more and more of just those items – for the biggest audience may not be, and mostly is not, the majority of the potential audience; even if it is, there will be minorities, often huge minorities, who have their own expectations; indeed the sum of minorities is at any given time normally larger than the 'majority' audience. Additionally, programmes provided for relatively small but intently engaged audiences may provide a greater sum of enjoyment than others addressed to very large but indifferent audiences. And finally, if audience ratings are the determining factor, the new and unusual will not be shown.

All these considerations should be a guard against esteeming television as a god of infinite power rather than as one public servant among many, and against dogmatic statements about the aims and influence of the broadcasting services. Radio and television are a potent supplement to, not a substitute for, more traditional kinds of communication, recreation and instruction. The value of broadcasting services compared with other social services needs to be kept under review, as well as the charge they make upon the public purse and their effects upon other instruments of communication and public institutions. It is possible, for example, that radio and television might consume money, technical skills and resources, human energy and ingenuity, out of all proportion to their worth in com-

**Sociology in Mass Communication* (Penguin, 1972).

†See Alasdair Clayre, *Broadcasting and Society* (Fifth Symposium on Broadcasting Policy, 1973, Manchester University).

parison with other social, commercial and educational undertakings. It is possible, and some would confidently assert, that there is too much television, and that it distracts many people from other more humanly satisfying and socially useful activities. Broadcasting could conceivably silence alternative sources of information and stimulation which require more effort on the part of the user but which provide more thorough knowledge or more intense pleasure. There is some evidence to suggest that television has in fact altered social habits and modified the relationship between the public and the politicians who are subjected, as never before, to intimate scrutiny. On the other hand, many beneficial effects have been claimed. These range from keeping people off the streets in dangerous circumstances such as exist in Ulster, to increasing the sales of books and technical magazines or the popularity of minority sports, to providing workers in heavy industry with relaxation of a richness and diversity hitherto undreamed of. However, in the judgement of the Commission, the relationship between television and particular social phenomena still belongs, on the whole, to the realm of speculation and much thoroughgoing research is needed before the exact nature of this relationship is demonstrated in detail. Given the importance to society of knowing how it is affected by television, it is regrettable that social science research into the influence of mass communicators, of the kind currently being conducted in university cèntres of investigation at Leeds, Leicester and London, is still the Cinderella of the communications industry, and one of our firmest conclusions is that such research should be given a high priority both by Government and by the broadcasting institutions themselves. At present, partisan armies meet upon the field of television to exchange fusillades of prejudicial generalities. There is a need for proven particularities so that public and producers alike may have more to go on.

Setting goals for a broadcasting service and assessing its achievements are difficult tasks not only because there is insufficient hard evidence concerning the relationship between stated objectives and actual effects on the viewer or listener, but also because a broadcasting service overlaps so many other professions and services: journalism, entertainment, education and so forth. As Howard Newby, now Director of Programmes, BBC Radio, has said: 'Counsel about radio and television is repeatedly darkened by arguments appropriate to quite different matters . . . radio and television are not producers in an industrial sense and they are something more than organs of information and opinion.' Thus the economic argument that competition leads to lower prices and a better service to consumers, or the view, drawn from the Press and publishing, that freedom requires competition and the absence of central control, are not necessarily pertinent to a broadcasting service. Competition for scarce talent and resources increases costs and without some kind of central control to counterbalance the magnetic pull of entertainment and hectic pursuit of maximal audiences, does not inevitably lead to a wider choice for listeners and viewers. Nor does it follow that the public will be best served by a ceaseless multiplication of broadcasting sources. The analogy between broadcasting and the publishing of books or newspapers is not, in our views, an exact one. There is no theoretical limit to the number of books and newspapers which is desirable and individuals benefit from a wide range of choice to suit their tastes and interests. There is, however, a limit to the number of people which even a bestseller or the most popular newspaper will actually reach. Broadcasting, on the other hand, is currently limited by shortage of airspace, yet in practice can reach an unlimited audience. It is therefore, though naturally incapable of providing the same depth of treatment as a book or newspaper, able to undertake tasks which they cannot. Notably, it can convey to the mass of the nation those matters which are of most importance to the mass of the nation, and provide a shared experience which no other medium of communication can supply. This is a telling argument for maintaining national networks and against multiplying broadcasting services simply because they are technically feasible or commercially profitable. National networks cannot, however, claim a monopoly of the public's attention, and to carry the argument to the point of excluding additional local services or multiple services which are technically possible would, we feel, be going too far. A balance has to be struck between the value of experiences and information shared in common by the mass audience, whether through a comedy programme, a news bulletin, or a documentary – all of which in various ways can forge a subtle bond between disparate elements in society – and the respectful and careful consideration which must be given to individual, local and regional interests. In deciding where to strike the balance, the criteria of competition and cost effectiveness are not the sole considerations.

The task of setting goals for the broadcasting services is therefore a difficult one. This does not mean that it should not be attempted, nor that the goals which have served adequately in the past should not be further refined and improved on, provided that the complexity of a broadcasting service is constantly borne in mind, its limitations understood, and the fact registered that such aims are pursued within a particular social context. Those who work in broadcasting do not operate in a social vacuum and they have only as much room for manœuvre as the values and purposes of society as a whole allow them.

Although it is difficult to determine the precise effects of broadcasting on individuals and on society, there is a natural presumption that since the broadcasting services attract so much time and attention, their influence must be considerable. In Maurice Edelman's words: 'It has been established in the United States that a child who has reached the age of 18 has spent 20,000 hours viewing television and about 10,800 hours at school. That is a measure of the instructive quality of television and is a measure of the impact of television.'* The figures for Great Britain must be roughly comparable and no stronger motive could be proposed for continually assessing the effects of television and setting goals which will enrich and not impoverish the public for whose benefit broadcasting services are provided.

Both the BBC and the IBA are charged by Parliament with the duty of providing services which inform, educate and entertain. This formula has become the classic definition of the aims to be pursued under the general heading of 'public service'. It is based on three considerations. First, that any declaration of aims must be capable of translation into the structural terms which govern decision-making within the broadcasting organisations. These organisations determine the means, but the ends are determined by the changing pressures of opinion in society at large and formulated by Government in the Act and Charter. There must be broad working instructions which are clear, unambiguous and capable of being implemented without too much wrangling about their terms. If they lay too great a burden of interpretation on the Governors, they would reinforce central controls, be inoperable at the production level which is the hub of a broadcasting service, and create misunderstandings between producers and public. Second, that these three categories of broadcasting are sufficiently wide for professional broadcasters to consider every aspect of human life as within their ambit. Third, that a broadcasting service should provide viewers and listeners with the widest range of subject matter from which to choose – choice, that is, between programmes which differ in subject matter, seriousness and stylistic treatment. There is no point in multiplying the sources of broadcasting if the programmes to be seen and heard differ very little in kind. As Parliament put it in Section 1(4)(b) of the Television Act

**Hansard*, col. 1521, 3 May 1973.

of 1964, the programmes are to maintain a high general standard in all respects, and in particular in respect of their content and quality, and a proper balance and wide range in their subject matter, having regard both to the programmes as a whole and also to the days of the week on which, and the hours of the day at which, the programmes are broadcast. Both Government and Opposition expected the broadcasting authorities to interpret this specification in a spirit which would 'respect the public's right to choose from the widest possible range of subject matter and so to enlarge worthwhile experience'.*

Viewed against this background, the traditional triad of information, education and entertainment appears, and in practice has proved, to be a flexible and workable statement of aims. It is understood by both professional organisations and the public. Within it the broadcasting institutions have found scope for adaptation and change to meet changing circumstances. It has by its very existence and its liberal nature discouraged any temptation to think of broadcasting services as instruments of propaganda – whether social, cultural or political – so matching the formula that the broadcasting institutions should be autonomous in their day-to-day operations, but not entitled to editorialise on their own account, which is a built-in defence against their engaging in systematic propaganda. At the same time the traditional definition of aims is not perfect. Its weakness is that information, education and entertainment are not clear-cut categories: programmes billed as entertainment can be informative and educative, and education and information register more effectively if put over in an entertaining way. Entertainment, indeed, must not be decried – not least because the 'serious' uses of television depend on it for their very life. As the first aim of a newspaper is to be read, so the first aim of a broadcasting service is to be listened to or watched. Before high purposes can be achieved there must be an audience, and in practice it is entertainment which attracts an audience. But leaving even this consideration aside, entertainment has a value in itself. It answers a deeply felt human need and is a necessary element in a broadcasting service that has the good of 'the whole man' in view. Both radio and television have in fact made a greater quantity and better quality of entertainment available to everyone, introduced all to kinds of entertainment which were once the monopoly of a particular class, and brightened many lives which without it would be drab and circumscribed. What needs to be resisted, however, is the strong gravitational pull of entertainment, whether it takes the form of a disproportionate allotment of time to 'pure'

Hansard, cols 105–8, 14 March 1963.

entertainment, or, probably worse still in the long run, of trivialising serious matters by the relentless application of 'showbiz' values. If facts are distorted or misused for the sake of colourful treatment, if serious issues are entrusted to lively but ill-informed speakers, if complex questions are over-simplified, if disciplined thought is neglected, if questions which have puzzled mankind for centuries are rationed to a few moments' discussion, the results may be entertaining but the educative and informative results positively harmful.

A further weakness of the formula is that it is primarily concerned with benefits to the individual and only indirectly with its effects on society as a whole, whereas growing awareness of broadcasting as an instrument of social change is increasingly raising questions about the social purposes to which it can be directed for the common good, and the effects which it may unintentionally produce if not so directed. This raises the question of ultimate purposes, not only for broadcasting as such but for society as a political, social and cultural entity. It is not the task of those who control or work in broadcasting, nor have they the right, to determine what is meant by 'the good life', 'the good man', or to mount an institutional challenge to whatever understanding of the national interest is embraced by the democratically elected Parliament. But those on the producing end of broadcasting must in practice have some guiding star if they are to judge what kinds of information, education and entertainment are to be transmitted.

Information for what? Education for what? Entertainment for what? Even to dodge such questions involves theoretical judgements, perhaps lying unexpressed beneath the surface, about the nature of man and the nature of society, judgements which underly day-to-day practical decisions about which programmes are worth doing, how they are to be done and what they intend to achieve. Furthermore, if there is no unifying vision, shared in common by those who operate the broadcasting services, there is no guarantee that the sum of random effects will not be a view of man and a kind of society which no responsible person would deliberately have chosen to foster.

Is it possible, then, for there to be a unifying vision in a society which is politically, culturally and socially fragmented, shared by the whole of society and professional broadcasting staff as members of society, sufficiently broad to allow for wide divergences of personal creeds and convictions, yet not so vague as to be useless in practice? For certainly any notion of using the broadcasting services, as they are used in some countries, to impose government policy, a political ideology or religious faith, would run clean contrary to the tolerance demanded in a pluralist society as well as the constitutional traditions of the broadcasting institutions themselves.

With regard to the use of broadcasting as an instrument of social change, perhaps the time has come for it to be employed more consciously and deliberately to serve the interests of participatory democracy. The broadcasting services, television especially, should not be regarded as a threat to, or substitute for, the Law and Parliament, but a useful complement and ally in pursuing the social aims of justice and democratic participation. Those who run television cannot take political and social decisions on behalf of the people but they can greatly assist people to make the best possible contribution to the decisions made on their behalf by their elected representatives. Similarly, television must not become a court of law as it threatened to do when Emile Savundra and later John Petro were virtually tried by television (*The Frost Programme*, 1967 and 1968), but it can spotlight abuses of law or weaknesses in the law itself, or unfair practices in commercial, social and governmental institutions. As a social instrument it is well fitted to equip people to be more responsible citizens and exercise more say over their own lives. It can do this in a number of ways:

i) It can inform people of the issues of the day, the choices available, the various ways of achieving results, and the part they themselves can play.
ii) It can be a forum of debate on the goals of society, and analyse the existing social institutions.
iii) It can explore gaps and breakdowns in the social services, reveal what needs to be done and how results can be achieved.
iv) It can assist specialist groups to acquire skills which are of value to society.
v) It can provide richer entertainment for many who in times past had few opportunities to enjoy their leisure.
vi) It can break down isolation and be a solace to the lonely.
vii) It can provide knowledge and encourage sympathetic understandings of unfamiliar ways of life, beliefs and customs.
viii) It can enlarge the common stock of experience which in many subtle ways develops a sense of unity between people.
ix) In a special way, it can give a voice to the voiceless and limelight to the obscure.
x) It can supplement inadequate formal education and in certain circumstances add a new dimension to learning by enabling people to watch themselves engaged in the process of learning.

The broadcasting services do in fact already attempt most of these tasks with varying degrees of success but it is still worth highlighting the value of television as a social instrument, both because the right of the broadcasting services to probe political and social issues has only slowly won acceptance, and because this social role has a bearing on the types of broadcasting which are desirable. Communication is the life-blood of any community, but especially a community as complex as our own. Population growth, social mobility, the remoteness of powerful political and commercial institutions which affect almost everybody's life, the ramifications of bureaucracy, the difficulty of understanding advanced science and technology, all these and many other factors bewilder and cause frustration to many people, and make them feel they have little control over the circumstances of their lives. Whether it is saving the street they live in from developers, getting traffic signals at a dangerous crossing, deciding whether Maplin Airport, the Channel Tunnel or Concorde are desirable, what social services are needed and how they can be improved – whether the issues are large national ones or small local ones intimately affecting daily life – there is a strong feeling that more factual information is needed in an intelligible form, together with a better understanding of the options, and more comprehension of the way in which Government works. Television has an as yet unrealised capacity to lighten this darkness. Already opinion polls (e.g. a survey by the Centre for Mass Communication Research, University of Leicester) suggest that half the population rely on it for news and information, and trust it more than any other medium, presumably on the principle that seeing is believing.

Both the degree of public reliance on television news and the participatory principle, which should not be received as merely another pious platitude, have definite implications for policy in the field of news' and current affairs' programming. The participatory principle poses a challenge to the domination of such broadcasts by traditional news values, demanding that the amount of attention paid to topics be determined more by their significance than by their sensationalism. It requires the substitution of more analytical forms of presentation, where appropriate, for bitty, breathless and unconnected ones. It compels a re-examination of styles of treatment of issues and groups in the news that perpetuate uncritically accepted stereotypes. It calls for investigatory journalism, provided that the broadcasting services observe high standards of factual accuracy and allow all sides to be heard. And, above all, it is desirable that future Government decisions should be thoroughly aired in good time to enable the public to absorb the necessary information and make a judgement upon it.

With regard to the individual, the aim of the broadcasting services should be to bring about maximum personal enrichment, keeping the humanity of the viewer or listener at the forefront of the mind. On the one hand there is a tendency in modern society to view people under one aspect, as consumers, employers or employees, citizens, householders, electors, party members, or, in the case of television and radio, as actual or potential viewers and listeners. On the other, there is a sense of human qualities and talents which are running to waste, often for reasons outside the control of the individual. Those who control and operate the broadcasting services must be primarily concerned with the whole human being, with providing, as far as in them lies, the means of awakening dormant human qualities and talents. This may seem to be a vague concept and to impose an unreasonable moral obligation on those who direct broadcasting services, but its practical implications can be spelled out more clearly. First of all, even allowing for the divergencies that exist as to what is and what is not acceptable human behaviour, what are and what are not the ideal human qualities, what beliefs and behaviour go to the making of a fully human being, there is still a consensus of agreement about what is human and what is inhuman. Cruelty, dishonesty, rampant greed, selfishness and heartlessness are all examples of qualities which, however common, are generally regarded as unworthy of the truly human being. Compassion, generosity, honesty, tolerance and consideration for others are generally regarded as highly desirable human qualities. As far as the broadcasting services are concerned, both in their own manner of operation and in the general tenor of their programmes, there should be the utmost concern to illuminate and foster the highest human ideals. This is especially true with regard to the cumulative influence of television. Of course a television service which ignored and failed to explore the dark and disagreeable aspects of human life as it is actually lived would be a dishonest service; the complexity and ambiguities of human behaviour must also be honestly respected. But a good television service will be one which avoids patterns of programming that involve a gross distortion of the human values people uphold and care for. Individual programmes are less important in this respect than the diet as a whole. For example, however exiguous the scientific evidence may be, it is still difficult to believe that a constant diet of programmes in which both heroes and villains alike use violent methods to achieve their ends and in which life is held cheap does not eventually blur the distinction between ends and means, increase the likelihood of ruthless behaviour and diminish respect for life. Similarly, although the broadcasting services cannot be blamed for a materialistic spirit in society at large, those who control broadcasting should be aware that it may intensify this spirit by providing a diet of programmes identifying human happiness with material possessions or glamorising the rich and powerful with little regard for the ways in which the riches and power have been obtained, or the uses to which they are put. Another practice which may be harmful in the long run is an excessive use of film stars and light entertainment personalities even in serious discussion programmes. Certainly they are highly paid and attract an, often carefully cultivated, public attention, but there seems no good reason for the broadcasting services to encourage the notion that their views on all kinds of topics have a peculiar validity. On the other hand, it is possible that programmes like *Family Favourites*, the *Terry Wogan Show* or *Late Night Extra*, by their friendliness, good humour, sympathy for people in distress and by putting friends and relatives in touch one with another, do far more than is generally appreciated to foster warm and kindly feelings. In short, the cumulative effect of various species of broadcasting in building up public attitudes, values and heroes, is far more important than the shock effect of a single programme like *The Operation* or *Hell's Angels* or the David Bailey film about Andy Warhol, which quickly vanish into 'the dark backward and abysm of time'. In respect of human values, British series like *Softly, Softly*, *Sutherland's Law* or *Callan* seem to many people better than American crime and adventure series; subtler and more imaginative in their understanding of human nature, with better characterisation, dialogue, settings, more varied plots and far less violence. Especially during peak viewing hours the home-grown product deserves preference on both artistic and moral grounds and these should have a higher priority than any purely economic consideration. This is worth saying because the proportion of American imports during peak hours actually exceeds the stipulated 14 per cent.

Such moral considerations range beyond the boundaries of broadcasting but the potential educative effect of television and radio is so great that we believe broadcasting must be at least as concerned about the moral influence of programmes, as well as cultural, artistic and technical standards, as are schools and other educational institutions. By morality we mean the good of the whole person, not merely the puritanical sexual mores which are often wished upon the broadcasters. At production level the integrity with which programmes are made in all their aspects – research, selection of participants, technical standards and the avoidance of any kind of gimmickry – is itself a moral influence. And at the administrative level the same moral concern should have regard to the all-round human good of the public rather than narrow institutional interest. Undoubtedly this raises problems which admit no easy solution, but they are problems that ought to be honestly faced. It may be, for example, that it is in the institutional interest to use every endeavour to catch and hold the largest possible audience, but that the continuous viewing which would result might create an addiction harmful to the viewer as a person. Recent studies in Germany (Munich Society for Rational Psychology, 1971) suggest that such addiction may in fact occur. But if what is at present mainly speculation proved in fact to be something truly harmful to society and the person, even the severest measures like limiting the hours of viewing or closing down the service at intervals could not be ruled out. In this respect, too, the social context within which the broadcasting services operate is seen to be crucial.

In 1958, Edward R. Murrow wrote of television: 'This instrument can teach, it can illuminate; yes, and it can even inspire. But it can only do so to the extent that humans are determined to use it to those ends. Otherwise it is merely lights and wires in a box.' Britain has been fortunate that a sense of moral purpose has been built into the broadcasting institutions. They have been lucky too in being allowed to work out their own purpose and method. They have thus avoided the authoritarianism of Eastern European or French television and the blatant commercialisation of American stations. But only constant vigilance, public debate and criticism, and reassessment of goals, will prevent television from being 'merely lights and wires in a box'. It is out of respect for the medium as a serious informant and educator that we wish its goals to be given a sharper focus and explicit social objectives, not from any wish to restrict its subject matter or inhibit those who work in broadcasting. On the contrary we want the whole panorama of human life to fall under its gaze; but to be so studied, interpreted and transmitted to the public, that all who use television may be helped to achieve their highest human potential, and society be gradually improved to the point where every man is free to be human.

2 THE STRUCTURES OF BROADCASTING

Once it has been decided what broadcasting can and should do, it is necessary to consider the means. The organisation of broadcasting differs from country to country, partly as a result of local historical circumstances but also because in every country the government has created or allowed a broadcasting system which it calculates will serve the national interest. In many countries, totalitarian governments exercise strict control over broadcasting, which is viewed primarily as a propaganda medium. In others, such as the United States, radio and television services are run almost entirely by commercial interest, solely for shareholders with only occasional government intervention. In Western Europe most countries have aimed to strike a balance between central government control and unchecked commercialisation. In Great Britain, the British Broadcasting Corporation is a unique invention created by Royal Charter as a public service which was 'not to be a department of the State, still less a creature of the executive'* but a trustee for the national interest, ultimately responsible to the public through the elected Parliament, and entirely independent in the day-to-day conduct of its affairs. Out of this mechanism, designed to reconcile independence with responsibility, has developed a broadcasting institution with an un-

*Government spokesman in House of Commons debate, 1926.

paralleled worldwide reputation for high technical and programme standards, a doctrine of good broadcasting recognised by both the broadcasting organisations and the general public, and a sense of public service as the chief aim of those who administer and engage in broadcasting. Even when the BBC monopoly was broken and commercial television introduced, these basic assumptions about the independence of broadcasting authorities and the character of good broadcasting had taken such a strong hold that they were written into the Constitution of the IBA by Act of Parliament.

There is, therefore, an inter-relationship between public needs, Parliament, and the broadcasting institutions, and the latter have come into being as a result of certain assumptions concerning needs, ideas and practical possibilities. As changes take place in society, these assumptions may also alter and the broadcasting institutions themselves feel the need to change in order to undertake whatever new tasks are expected of them. They may require expansion, contraction, adjustment, demolition or renovation. Technical innovations may also alter the context in which broadcasting institutions have traditionally worked, and modify in some respects the relationship between them and their public. Yet it is not easy to identify the social changes which require a flexible response, or for institutions of any kind to cast off ingrained habits and traditions and adopt new directions and methods except under pressure from the outside. On the whole, we believe the broadcasting institutions have proved themselves more responsive than might have been expected, and this makes it possible to be optimistic about their future. Notwithstanding the fact that some critics believe the whole present structure of broadcasting in this country should be entirely rebuilt, we favour a policy of gradual reform which will retain what is best in our broadcasting traditions, yet be open to experiment and new patterns in programming.

In the first part of our Report we have mentioned some of the social changes which have occurred and how these have influenced radio and television services: cultural fragmentation, changes in attitudes towards authority, the desire for political and social democratic participation, the growing complexity of a modern industrialised society. To these can be added increased social mobility, improvements in the quantity and quality of mass education, a distinctive youth culture, material affluence, greater sensitivity to environmental hazards and to the quality of life – all previously unknown features of British society and all of them to a greater or lesser extent bringing about new demands on the broadcasting system. So also do technological developments like cablevision, videotape cassettes and satellite broadcasts, all of which could in the foreseeable, though not immediate, future lessen the influence of the national networks. Changes and developments such as these, some of them induced or speeded up by the medium itself, are already prompting questions about the broadcasting institutions as they exist. Are they not doing things which need to be done? If incapable, is this because of inherent and unalterable characteristics or because of external influence over which they have no control? Do the new technological developments spell the end of national broadcasting systems as we know them? It is with these questions that this section of our Report is concerned.

Of the two broadcasting institutions in the United Kingdom, the BBC is universally regarded as the best broadcasting organisation in the world. It has established a philosophy of broadcasting and created professional broadcasting standards which have worldwide influence. In Sir Hugh Greene's words: 'It is internationally accepted that the BBC provides the best broadcasting and is the most efficient and economically run broadcasting organisation in the world. It is the subject of constant study by other broadcasting organisations.'* The BBC has continually advanced technical standards and its training programmes have produced a steady stream of men and women who carry its ideals and standards into broadcasting services both at home and abroad. It constantly attracts and cultivates a vigorous community of gifted people. Its outposts around the world provide a news and information service of high quality. It has been a generous and enlightened patron of the Arts, both spokesman and showman for Britain, and rendered an inestimable service to education in the United Kingdom. Certainly in the heyday of radio broadcasting, on which the BBC built its reputation, it expressed a liberal outlook and a respect for civilised rational discourse which have influenced public standards. The fact has been noted by McQuail in a recent interview that: 'Broadcasting has introduced almost universally in Britain the same criteria of what is true and valid and what is evidence.'†

While it enjoyed a monopoly, the BBC provided, especially during the war years, a common experience; both its serious programmes and light entertainment became a staple of conversation shared in by all classes and varieties of people and almost certainly contributed to

*Granada Guildhall Lecture, 1972.
†'Forming or Informing', prog. 4 of *The Impact of Broadcasting*, BBC-Radio 3, 27 October 1972.

the sense of national unity and national community. Even nowadays the tendency remains for people to turn to the BBC for coverage of extraordinary events and at moments of national crisis. Finally, it is worth remarking that despite much mockery of the BBC for its supposed upper-middle-class tone and mild pomposity, its audience was and is largely made up of people with limited formal education to whom it has made accessible a wide range of skills and knowledge.

The arrival in 1954 of commercial television, with its greater need for mass audiences, changed the framework of television broadcasting in Britain, and indirectly affected the Corporation. The Pilkington Report of 1962 saw the early days of independent television as marked by a scramble for ratings and a sharp decline in programme standards (though television drama, in which ABC Television pioneered new ideas, was a notable exception). Franchises were withdrawn from two of the commercial companies in 1967. These events, together with an inherited regard for programme standards among those who work for the companies, and eventually a kind of tacit gentleman's agreement between the BBC and the IBA to go halves in the national audience rather than fight each other to the death, led to a gradual but substantial improvement in the quality and balance of programmes. It is argued by some that too much hack-work, much of it imported, still reaches the screen, but it is also true that independent television news, current affairs and documentary programmes are often as good as, if not better, than the BBC's, and that certain series, for example Anglia's *Survival*, Granada's *Country Matters* and *State of the Nation* or London Weekend's *Upstairs Downstairs* would do credit to any television service.

Maurice Edelman has observed 'There is a kind of symbiosis between commercial television and the BBC. One organisation tends to assimilate itself to the other.'* There is a good deal of truth in this statement and it would be a welcome notion if it meant that each organisation assimilated the best features of the other. But this will only happen if and when both organisations are concerned with good broadcasting exclusively, and that in turn will only happen if the tyranny of the ratings is broken. Freedom from outside pressure, whether from Government, advertisers, company shareholders, or any other direction, does not guarantee that broadcasting organisations will make uniformly excellent programmes, but without such freedom there is a greater danger that undeserving programmes will

**Hansard*, col. 1517, 3 May 1973.

reach the screen. The independence of the broadcasting authorities from Government intervention has now become part of the country's unwritten constitution and a similar independence from intervention by commercial interests, not exclusively concerned with programme standards, must be defended.

Advertisers very naturally wish to catch and hold the largest possible audience and to present commercials where programmes have built up such an audience. This leads to strict scheduling, programmes in the early part of the evening which are more or less guaranteed to hook a large audience, rigid time-slots, regular series which establish a viewing habit, but above all to an emphasis on undemanding, unprovocative entertainment during peak hours (that is, approximately from 7 p.m. until 10 p.m.). This simple and successful formula for maximising audiences has been imitated in its turn by the BBC, which has reduced the variety of programming during peak hours, and fought independent television on its own ground of crime-thriller-espionage series, variety, panel-games and feature films, while trying to do them better. Only the existence of its second channel has allowed peak-hour minority interest programmes driven out of the front door to return by the back (though audience inertia which inhibits switching over from one channel to another and straitened finances have militated against the kind of adventurousness originally expected of BBC 2).*

Summarising the gains and losses which have resulted from the coming of commercial television broadcasting is not easy, since no one can say with certainty which improvements would still have taken place if it had not existed. Among the indubitable gains is the creation of more job opportunities and alternative employment for those who work in broadcasting. The first Director General of IBA, Sir Robert Fraser's ingenious invention of a system of regional television companies, to foster competition, has strengthened the sense of regional character and loyalty, especially in the provinces. Individual companies have been originators within their own particular specialisations: ATV, for example, in certain kinds of light entertainment, Granada in tackling social issues, Thames in current affairs, Yorkshire in drama series. The existence of independent television has at least speeded up the removal of finicky restrictions on political discussion. And although commercial

*A lively account of this process of assimilation since the summer of 1957 when the BBC's share of the audience was 27 per cent to the Independent Television's 73 per cent can be found in Peter Black's *The Mirror in the Corner* (Hutchinson), p. 136.

competition has narrowed the range of programme variety within peak hours, it has stimulated the BBC to higher standards of performance within that range. As for the losses, the chief of these, once again, is the narrowing of choice at those times when it is most convenient for people to watch. The showbusiness approach to programmes has generally been accentuated even when the desire to be bright works against a full, serious and accurate description of facts, a complete spectrum of viewpoints, and comprehensive discussion. When an occasional programme does allow participants to express their views at length, and argument to run its full course, as does Thames's *Something to Say*, it is consigned to an hour likely to suit only insomniacs and night-watchmen.

Competition has also pushed up the costs of television. In the year ending March 1955 the BBC spent £5 m. on its television service – today it spends £73,730,000. Expansion of services, general inflation and the introduction of colour account for much of this increase, but another reason is certainly competition for scarce talent and skills, and monopoly rights. Commercial pressure for more hours of television broadcasting, largely to reach the housewife with daytime advertising, has multiplied low-cost, low-quality programmes and indirectly strained BBC resources; for our impression is that the Corporation would prefer to spend its money on high-quality programmes for a shorter period of the day. The horse-trading between the five major independent television companies who compete for a share of time available on the national network, hinders the showing of more frequent imaginative and original programmes at peak hours, and severely restricts the opportunities open to the ten smaller companies of gaining access to a national audience. The system also favours rigid time-slots and long-running series, usually in groups of thirteen programmes, which are only reluctantly halted if they prove to be of poor quality. The rigid time-slot leads to artificial constraint on, for example, the length of plays, as well as to indefensible practices like making cuts in feature films. But perhaps the worst danger is of settling for the proven success, the predictable, the cosy, the routine, of avoiding experiment because of programme companies' fears that audiences will fall and advertisers' patience run out, and of requiring instant success or a quick death instead of allowing a genuinely original programme idea to create a taste and accumulate an audience over a period of time. It is not surprising that even in the field of popular entertainment, where the commercial companies expected a walk-over (and despite undoubted successes like London Weekend's

Upstairs Downstairs, Thames's *Callan*, Granada's *A Family at War* and *The Comedians*), the BBC's situation comedies like *Steptoe and Son* or *Dad's Army*, or series such as *Softly, Softly*, *Elizabeth R* and *Dr Finlay's Casebook*, have consistently attracted a greater meed of critical praise for their imaginative invention and quality of characterisation.

Some of the BBC's troubles, as we have seen, are the result of pressures which it cannot resist if it is to survive, but induce schizophrenia, at least in the minds of those reared in the pre-independent television tradition. If it does not attract at least 40 per cent of the national audience it becomes vulnerable to the charge that those who pay the licence fee are paying for an institution whose services they do not use. Yet to retain the mass audience which justifies its existence the BBC must often pursue policies in which, in the depths of its heart, it does not believe. It is asked, indeed commanded, to aim at quality, inventiveness, variety of choice, rather than simply to satisfy popular taste, yet does not enjoy all the necessary freedom to achieve this aim as well as it could. Its limited resources are, moreover, dispensed among a multitude of local, regional, national and international services. Another pressure comes from irreconcilable public attitudes: some see it as a commercial organisation which should pay its way or perish, others as an austere monastic community where truth, beauty and virtue can be pursued without thought of worldly gain; others again as the shrine containing the national Lares and Penates; some see it as a venerable sage instructing the nation in wisdom and virtue, others as a haunt of juvenile anarchists and delinquents bent on shaking the pillars of the kingdom; some consider it or wish it to be the voice of the establishment, others the establishment's severest critic. Institutions, like men, play in their time many parts – neither can be expected to play all at once.

To some extent it is the BBC's perennial financial problem which creates the aggressive defensiveness that is one of its notorious failings. When the BBC does not do things well, or fails to do what it ought to do, its own professional staff are as well positioned to know it as outside critics, and are sometimes quite plainly galled by the knowledge that it is not lack of good intentions or ability but lack of money which is often the cause. If the BBC is expected by Parliament to provide programmes which are not necessarily the most popular, but certainly in the national interest, then the means should be provided. We believe that increases in the licence fee should be regarded as the necessary price of a public service vital to the public interest and be sufficient to relieve the BBC of excessive financial anxiety.

On another flank, attacks come from critics who believe that the BBC is too large and unwieldy. This too is a charge which does not stand up to examination. By industrial standards it is not a particularly large concern, certainly not too large for efficient management. On the contrary, the fact that it is centrally controlled, embraces radio and television, foreign and domestic services, and can build up permanent units and teams which specialise within the whole range of programme species – news, drama, current affairs and so forth – is one of its major strengths. This can, and often does, lead to valuable cross-fertilisation between departments, a degree of internal competitiveness, a permanent store of experience in each department, an ethos, a way of doing things, a 'house style', which are absorbed by those in its employ. Those who work in the commercial companies know that this flexibility and hoarded experience are beyond emulation by a smaller broadcasting organisation, though it is true that for some people the atmosphere and less formal relationships of the smaller organisation may prove more congenial. Institutions, however, almost inevitably lapse into institutionalism, and a more valid criticism of the BBC comes under this head. Some within the Corporation argue that too many production decisions are made at an administrative level instead of by the producer directly responsible for the programme and that these decisions are swayed by considerations other than the objective merits of a programme. There seems to be some substance in this criticism. But once a public institution dedicated to the public service becomes a self-preservation society, life gradually drains out of it and it becomes moribund. If the BBC is perpetually to renew the springs of its vigour it will have to be at least as sensitive to this danger from within as to assaults from without. As for the charge that the BBC is secretive, this will be discussed in the third section of our Report.

Among various interest groups and organisations there is today a growing desire to have direct access to the broadcasting media. They wish to present their activities and views in their own way and on their own terms, instead of having them presented at second-hand, or entirely ignored, by the broadcasting institutions. In principle, we believe that such access brings a new and valuable element into broadcasting, even though presentation may be amateurish by traditional standards. The practical difficulties, however, are considerable. Access on a large scale, given a limited number of frequencies, is virtually impossible, and there is also the problem of deciding who among many claimants are to be given airtime. For the present we would like to see both institutions providing at least one, and perhaps two, hours a week along the lines of the BBC's *Open Door* programme which has succeeded sufficiently to overcome initial scepticism and prompt a further series. We surmise that access programmes at weekends rather than in the late weekday hours might attract an even larger audience, and advise that some room should be made for them on the fourth channel, no matter to whom it is eventually allocated. But in the long term large-scale access will only prove practicable, and also in all probability prove most effective, as an ingredient of local and community services. Existing radio services are already gaining valuable experience in this field.

There is, however, a wider sense of access which should not be overlooked. To assume that the principle of access applies only to a few special programmes that have been deliberately moulded by it would be fallacious. In the more conventional news and current affairs programmes, it at least suggests a need to widen the range of spokesmen who are invited to air their views on issues of the day beyond the small circle of tried and trusty personalities who appear so regularly 'on the box'. And, of course, the more time that is allocated to a given subject, the more chance an individual spokesman will have of saying what he really thinks as distinct from what an interviewer wants to pin him down to.

Only a small minority of our Commission are opposed to television advertising in itself. The majority recognise that the money for a television service has to come from somewhere and that no alternative fairy godmother has yet appeared. Most also recognise that television advertising is subject to a strict code which is conscientiously and responsibly interpreted by the Authority. However, we would observe that the social and ethical questions which advertising raises are magnified by the dramatic quality of television and its potential social influence, and we would re-affirm the importance of studying how advertising in various subtle ways affects ideals and values. In his book *The Mirror in the Corner* (p. 184), Peter Black quotes an essay on advertising by Jacqueline Wheldon where she denounces 'the prejudice that is against all the difficult decencies of birth, love, age and meaningful death; against the complexities of judgements, taste, goodness, endurance and learned tolerance, the complexities of the absence of these things; against tunes that aren't jiggy, joys and loves that don't come instantly, cures that don't work quickly; against the value of pain, and bad weather, and discomfort; against the quality of life led by people who have learned to build into their lives great griefs and limitations of temperament and character'. There is sufficient truth peeping through this rhetoric to warrant close attention to the values insistently projected through advertising, and whether or not people unconsciously accept them or become resistant. The IBA cannot be held responsible for the advertising ethic that society as a whole tolerates, but it should certainly use its negative power to prevent systematic depreciation of higher values and exploitation of deeper human feelings and relationships – the intimate relationship between mother and child, for example. Suggesting that providing a particular brand of food is a serious test of a mother's love is an example of emotional blackmail which should be firmly discouraged in television advertising. Our Commission also recommends further exploration of different ways of regulating advertising, including restrictions to one period of an evening, or to intervals between programmes. The German system, which strictly regulates advertising before 8 p.m., and forbids it after that hour, while still attracting substantial advertising revenue, is especially to be noted.

Our overall view of the present broadcasting institutions is that they are well equipped to provide high-quality services and do in fact provide a range of choice which can be commended. One weakness common to both institutions is their incapacity to conduct long-term, in-depth research into the social influence of radio and television. It is arguable that this is not their task so much as that of the universities and other independent centres of investigation, but the broadcasting authorities at least have an obligation strongly to support work of this kind, both financially and through access to all forms of relevant information at their disposal. The BBC suffers from a chronic shortage of money and anxieties about its future financing: we believe that the licence fee, which is at present one of the lowest in Europe, could and should be raised whenever there is a serious danger of services being curtailed or programme standards reduced through lack of finance, and that other forms of financing such as grants for particular services should be explored, since it is the quality and tone of the public service system which sets the tone of the whole. On the other hand, we would welcome a greater willingness on the part of the BBC to be more open and less defensive in its relations with the public which finances it. Turning to the commercial system, we would welcome any measure strengthening the IBA's position vis-à-vis the companies. The Authority could, we think, play a greater part in the scheduling of programmes, build up the regional companies and ensure more time for their productions on the networks (at present their share of the time available on all the national networks is only 8 per cent), and provide development grants for experimental programmes. It should also insist on a higher percentage of genuinely serious programmes and reduce the percentage of imported products at peak viewing time. Much of this the IBA can (and some of it the Authority already does) achieve by charging lower rentals than it would otherwise have done to companies deserving what are, in effect, negative subsidies: e.g. the smaller regional companies and Harlech Television with its special commitment to Welsh language programmes. But in our view, the IBA should have the power and duty to provide positive subsidies directed to the improvement of its programmes. In addition, taking into account the high level of profits made by the companies in recent years, we think there is no justification for companies lagging behind in the provision of technical equipment or 'hardware'. Some, like Southern, have a good record in this respect, others are plainly deficient, a fact which has become more noticeable since the increase in programme hours. We also believe that both the BBC and IBA should buy in more work from independent producers to stimulate new approaches and ideas, and as long as their artistic and technical standards are met, even when this practice is not strictly economic. Finally, before the renewal of the Act and Charter, careful consideration should be given to foreign broadcasting systems with a view to adopting features which would improve the effectiveness of our own institutions and be in the public interest.

THE FOURTH CHANNEL

In the United Kingdom, airspace is available for six national television services, two on Very High Frequency (VHF) bands and four on the Ultra High Frequency (UHF) bands. This results from the Stockholm Agreement of 1961 which allocated VHF and UHF wavebands for European broadcasting, and allots four UHF television services to each country. The bandwidths allocated for television use in Europe are: Band I (VHF 41–68 MH), Band III (VHF 174–216 MH), Band IV (UHF 470–582 MH), and Band V (UHF 582–960 MH). At present UHF Bands IV and V carry BBC 1 and 2 and ITV on 625 lines. On these bands there is room for another national colour service usually referred to as TV 4. The VHF Bands I and III duplicate BBC 1 and ITV on 405 lines, but they cannot be released to carry new services until the approximately 10 per cent of British households which have only 405-line sets have replaced them with up-to-date models.* Therefore, although in theory the capacity for six television services exists, only one extra channel can in practice be activated until the mid-1980s when everyone is likely to have a 625-line set.

Whether to use TV 4, which exists only as a technical capacity, involves a political and social choice. Should it be used at all? Or is there any need for an extension of the existing television services? What good would it do? Who would control its use – BBC, IBA or some other agency? Does the public want it? And furthermore would the money needed for it (£30 m. to turn it on and about £30 m. more for annual running costs) be better spent on improving schools or the Health Service, or other social facilities? Many would argue that enough money is already spent on television services, and that there is already enough, if not too much, television for most people's needs. Only a political and social judgement based on thorough research and debate can decide whether they are right. Certainly the existing evidence, although slight, suggests that there is no overwhelming public demand for an extra television channel. Interviews with 589 people carried out at the end of 1972 by the Centre for Mass Communication Research at the University of Leicester indicated that 63 per cent were opposed to the idea of an additional channel, 33 per cent in favour, and that even those in favour wanted a different kind of service. More than 75 per cent of them wanted an extra channel to be used for specialised interests such as education and information programmes or cultural or hobbies programmes. When all respondents were presented with a series of alternative uses, 32 per cent opted for local television, 23 per cent for an education and information channel, and only 12½ per cent for more programmes of the kind they already get.

There are, however, many individuals and groups who feel that it would be wrong to let the fourth channel capacity lie idle, or that just because it exists, it will be allocated eventually, and therefore have formulated ideas on its use. Some schemes are fully worked out, others are embryonic. An outline of these schemes with the arguments for and against now follows:

A. ITV 2 – a scheme proposed by the IBA

Under this scheme the fourth channel would be operated by the

*Television Advisory Committee, 1972, Papers of Technical Sub-Committee, p. 20. (BREMA statistics.)

existing programme companies, providing a service complementary to ITV 1 with the IBA supervising programme planning schedules. It would be financed by advertising and the IBA suggests that the levy should be used in whole or part to finance the service. The IBA bases its claim on the supposition that competition on equal terms between the same services, IBA and BBC, each with complementary television channels, should improve the service given. A second channel would provide greater programming flexibility, more room for experimental and minority interest programmes, and to an extent relieve the frustrations of producers who at present cannot find scope for their ideas within a single channel. Time would be made available for access and educational programmes and for programmes submitted by independent producers. Those who favour this proposal do so largely because they believe it is the only one which can be adequately financed, is a way forward to strengthening the hand of the IBA in relation to the companies, could lead to a better balance in programming, and create more work for actors, directors, producers, writers and technicians. Against it are those who believe that the IBA has not yet proved its ability to fulfil its statutory obligations in regard to the companies, that it would result in two authorities which were simply mirror images of each other, and further increase the competition for audiences, the tendency of which is already to narrow choice, inflate costs and drive out educative and informational programmes from peak viewing hours. They also believe that an additional channel should be given to imaginative and experimental uses under the direction of a new agency, rather than provide more institutional television of the kind to which the public has grown accustomed, and are opposed to handing over a valuable public resource to an authority which is subjected, however subtly, to the pressure of private commercial interests.

B. A National Television Foundation

This proposal, the brainchild of Anthony Smith (Research Fellow of St Antony's College, Oxford, and former BBC producer) and adopted by the Association of Broadcasting Staff, is for a fourth channel to be run by a partly elected or representative body of trustees (appointed with the approval of the Minister of Posts and Telecommunications) and a small secretariat. It would be financed by grants from foundations and trusts, Parliament and Government agencies (including payment for special projects, e.g. programmes on education or environment) and from any other organisation wishing to sponsor particular programmes. The Foundation could commission work available for later sale, undertake joint projects with publishing organisations, buy in the best foreign- and home-produced programmes and, above all, attempt the kind of programme which the existing institutions either could not (e.g. because of their scheduling system) or would not attempt. Programmes would hopefully embody the aim of the NTF which is to initiate 'a new kind of private public debate in which the whole society is able to view the proceedings of its vital component elements'. In practice, this means offering both public bodies (e.g. the TUC or CBI) and private bodies, the chance to present their views to the public in their own chosen style and language, and at a length and on the occasions that they wish, instead of depending on the existing broadcasting institutions. The nub of the proposal is to introduce a Third Force into British broadcasting which proceeds from a different set of premises and does not compete on the same ground as the BBC and IBA, though seeking to respect traditional broadcasting standards.

In his Granada Guildhall lecture on 16 October 1972, Sir Hugh Greene favoured a partial adoption of the NTF to encourage experimental work for ITV 2. The NTF would be guaranteed adequate airtime, including some at peak hours, by the IBA, and the IBA would pay for programmes supplied by the NTF, but the NTF would be free to accept contributions from other sources. Other supporters have envisaged a marriage between the NTF and the IBA, or the NTF and the Open University or other educational bodies. The positive merits of the NTF proposal are that it adds a new but responsible source of energy and imagination to the present broadcasting services, would explore a different kind of relationship between broadcasters and audience, and experiment with different ways of balancing programmes and opinions within programmes. The main criticisms are that its system of finance would lend itself to domination by industry, since industrial companies could meet television costs too great for the pockets of most other social organisations, and Trusts would be an erratic and unreliable source of funds; that a greater degree of editorial control than the proposal seems to envisage would be necessary to meet broadcasting standards and ensure fair play, and that this would necessitate a larger staff than the mere skeleton crew proposed; that at least in its initial stages it could not provide a complete round-the-clock service; and that if it did in fact search out prospective programme-makers, it would have to adopt a system of programme scheduling which would quickly whittle away the time available for those spontaneous or open-ended programmes which are among its most attractive propositions.

On balance, however, it is an unusually imaginative proposal which deserves detailed and careful consideration.

C. Television 76 – a scheme proposed by the Institute of Practitioners in Advertising and the Incorporated Society of British Advertisers

This scheme proposes a broadcasting council with direct authority over (i) a public service sector incorporating a national special interest channel (BBC 2) plus BBC local radio and a fourth channel used for national social and educational programmes; (ii) a general interest television channel (BBC 1) financed by advertising and operated by a publicly owned corporation; (iii) a general interest television channel (ITV 1) financed by advertising and operated by appointed contractors; (iv) commercial radio. This scheme is self-confessedly prompted by the interests of the advertisers and has little else to recommend it since it is based on several presuppositions which lack support either inside or outside the broadcasting industry. There are, for example, strong arguments against a broadcasting council, set out in another section of this Report. The scheme would lead to commercial television taking over the two main mass audience channels, and to competition for advertising which is universally recognised as the surest way to lowering broadcasting standards. It would banish minority and special interest programmes to ghetto channels, and destroy the BBC as we know it. As Charles Curran remarked in a letter to *The Times* on 17 August 1973: 'The ISPA/IPA . . . suggest that the BBC has needlessly imposed on itself the duty to serve majorities . . . this is audacious nonsense, both historically and constitutionally.' It rests also on the fallacy that minority programmes are less expensive than popular programmes. In short, behind what is superficially a neat rationalisation of the broadcasting services, lies a wholesale change of strategy which would make the lowest common denominator in public taste influence the two major channels in a way which previous legislation on broadcasting has deliberately sought to avoid.*

D. Education services proposals

Various educationalists, such as Dr Walter Perry, Vice-Chancellor of the Open University, are anxious that the fourth channel should

*Following on the Government's decision to renew the Charter and the Act until 1981, the ISPA/IPA issued in September 1973 a revised interim proposal for the use of the fourth channel. This proposal aims to widen the programme appeal of ITV, increase the audience it reaches, introduce competition into the sale of advertising time and at the same time increase the supply of it available. It suggests increased opportunities for local and

carry Schools, Further Education and Open University programmes, possibly combined with an industrial education series to assist training in industry. This argument is based on the fact that there is not enough airspace at the present time for social and educational services, and that television has already proved its value as a teaching medium. Given room to expand, the educational services could provide a greater range of programmes for a greater number of specialised audiences at different levels of understanding than any other method and at lower cost. In terms of national needs such an educational channel invites strong support. There are, however, two difficulties, or rather qualifications, which need to be remarked: the present system of financing educational broadcasting would have to be changed, since so great an expansion would be beyond the means of the BBC, which has been the pioneer of educational broadcasting and whose non-involvement would be unthinkable; secondly, it would be undesirable for all educational programmes, no matter how general, to be confined in a single channel. The ideal might be for most straightforward teaching programmes for narrowly specialised audiences to be transmitted on the educational channel, leaving a good measure of generally educative programmes on the popular networks. Costs of educative programmes would then be borne by the BBC and the IBA. Costs of specialised educational programmes would be borne by the DES through a controlling agency, made up of the Open University, the Schools Broadcasting Council, the Further Education Advisory Council, etc., set up to administer funds and protect academic freedom.

E. A centrally scheduled national channel complementing ITV 1, proposed by John Birt and David Elstein

This envisages a centrally scheduled ITV 2 to provide balanced programming complementary to ITV 1. The channel would be run by a single programme controller with the balance supervised by the IBA. Programmes would be bought or commissioned from all sources including the present companies, and financed by advertising sold for both channels by the existing companies. The IBA would channel funds to ITV 2 either by imposing a levy on the companies

---

regional programming by means of stronger regional groupings, a wider choice of programmes both within and between channels, and improved efficiency in television advertising so that it becomes more competitive and more cost-effective and provides wider audience coverage. But *Television 76* remains the long-term definitive aim, and the objections outlined above still stand.

or by charging a secondary rental. This proposal aims to place the fourth channel under the charge of the IBA while avoiding competition between ITV 1 and ITV 2 for audiences and advertising. On the one hand the costs of the channel would be assured, on the other, good broadcasting could at least in theory be protected against commercial pressure. Against it is the argument that it is a compromise proposal which satisfies neither those who do not want the IBA to have an extra channel nor those who want an entirely new element brought into British broadcasting.

F. The BBC view

The BBC has made no bid for the fourth channel but it has expressed a view. It believes that all claims should be examined at leisure before the fourth channel is given away irretrievably to one purpose. It is opposed to the allocation of the fourth channel to IBA on the grounds that this would disturb the delicate balance between public and commercial services. It also holds that allocation should be for the satisfaction of a need at present unsatisfied rather than the expansion of choice for those who already enjoy it. The BBC does not wish to control a channel concerned with education or Welsh language transmission but would be willing to play a part in any consortium which the Government chose to set up to separate such broadcasting from the channels of both the BBC and the IBA. Behind the BBC view lies the supposition that some new agency will be needed to run a channel for diverse purposes, e.g. regional, educational and minority programmes, perhaps with some allocation of time to the NTF, and that no single proposal so far made would utilise the whole capacity of the fourth channel.

G. A publicly financed public service network modelled on the Swedish system

This would provide a second television channel competing with BBC 1 rather than complementing it as does BBC 2. This would provide a competitive vitality without the problem of programme quality raised by reliance on advertising revenue. It would also, as under the Swedish system, allow production staff a democratic say in programming and management. Critics claim that under the Swedish system, which requires one authority to oversee the two competing channels, the competitive edge is dulled and programme standards suffer.

H. Community television

It is argued that the falling cost of television equipment and the shorter range of the UHF transmitters would allow local educational authorities, technical colleges, universities and colleges of education which already own and run television facilities, and already produce more hours of programmes than either the BBC or IBA, to provide a flexible community television service, variously financed and programmed to suit local taste. All they would require would be facilities and Post Office approval for transmission. The main criticisms of this proposal are that its estimate of costs is over-optimistic, that production standards in the local institutions are still well below those to which the public are accustomed, and that an over-air network would be rapidly overtaken and made redundant by the anticipated development of cable television.

I. Other theoretical alternatives

Other proposals include a channel organised on the lines of the Dutch television system, which offers television facilities to any independent organisation that can prove it possesses an agreed level of support, and desires to put out its own programmes. The advantage of this proposal is that it would provide airspace for the full range of views which exist in a pluralist society. The disadvantage is that it could lead, as in Holland, to some kind of confessional television, with believers talking only to believers, and viewers watching only those programmes that fed their own prejudices.

A second theory is that the fourth channel should be devoted entirely to the proceedings of public bodies and Government, including local authority and Commons debates. The objection to this, apart from its cost, is that such a service would probably appeal mainly to the minority with the keenest interest in politics but already so actively involved that they would have little time to watch the programmes.

A third idea is that perhaps only one transmitter should be activated and used for a local service, perhaps in competition with a local cable service, so that costs, quality and effectiveness of the two services could be compared.

J. Independent Television Companies' proposal

The Independent Television Companies have, in the last few weeks, submitted to the Government their joint proposal for an ITV 2. As this has not yet been published, we have only very brief (but, we are informed, reliable) points to consider. The most notable feature is the Companies' outright support for a Third Force – a National Television Foundation – to be financed by the profits of the IBA Companies, commanding a considerable number of hours on the fourth channel, and administered by an Independent Programme Board. It is also conceded that more time should be given to regional minorities and national language groups, notably Welsh, with possible mergers of the small regional companies to facilitate this. The first of these proposals is a *volte face* by the Companies in as much as it would be yielding both time and money for programmes completely outside their control. But judgement will have to await more complete details of how much money, how many and what hours, etc., would be allocated.

It will be obvious from this list that some proposals contain only the germ of an idea and others are worked out in detail. Inevitably those proposals which contain carefully thought out ideas on structure, style of operation and financing are initially more persuasive, but it is possible that the at present sketchy, but more original, proposals might in the long run satisfy public needs that are as yet barely recognised and only occasionally articulated by a few prophetic voices.

The need to explore and weigh up the more speculative proposals is one reason why the decision to allocate the fourth channel should not be hurried, but other considerations tend to the same conclusion. The fourth channel is a valuable public resource and should be utilised to the best advantage of the public. Allocation of the fourth channel to one or other of the existing institutions will shut the door against experimental or other imaginative social uses for at least a decade. There is no strong public pressure for a quick decision, nor any discernible demand for a further expansion of the kind of services that already exist: this should create a bias in favour of employing the fourth channel for whatever new kinds of service are judged to be in the public interest. The proposals for devoting the fourth channel to regional, educational and local community needs, or a combination of these, have strong attractions and contain a good deal of sense in the light of general educational expansion. So too does the idea of creating a new agency to oversee the fourth channel and creating a new method of financing. But it is the view of our Commission that prolonged research and consideration is needed before answers can be confidently given to the large social questions which these proposals raise, as well as to the particular questions of organisation, control, access and finance. If, for example, public money is available to activate and run an extra television service, could it, would it and should it be spent on such a service in preference to other social services which are more urgently needed, or even perhaps the improvement of other communications systems? Or, if public money is to be put into an educational television channel, is it not at least possible that other educational services, for example the provision of nursery schools, have a stronger claim on available funds? There is no easy answer to these political and social questions but they deserve serious investigation and reflection before a new television service is brought into being.

In the light of the evidence it has received, our Commission has not been able to reach unanimous agreement on the allocation of the fourth channel other than that it should be kept in reserve until exhaustive feasibility studies have been made of all the proposals listed above. Some members would be willing to hand over the fourth channel to the IBA on condition that the Authority controlled the scheduling of programmes; that the Authority itself sold advertising time or otherwise controlled the allocation of advertising time on the second channel so that it would be under no obligation to attract the mass audience; and that the Authority provided airspace for independent producers. On the other hand, a majority of our Commission is opposed to extending the commercial services on the grounds that it is not convinced that the Authority has proved its ability to be master of the companies, that an ITV 2 mirror image of BBC 2 would be more likely to restrict choice than widen it, that it would disturb the balance of audiences between the BBC and IBA, and that, however good its intentions, the Authority would in the long run be able to offer very limited time and airspace to independent producers or minority groups. More positively, these members believe that the educational needs of the community have an overriding claim on the extra capacity afforded by the fourth channel. The success of the Open University shows how educational services could be extended to other sections of the community and make optimum use of scarce teaching resources. The details of such services are discussed in the fourth section of this Report. It is true that many people can only watch television at peak viewing times or at weekends but there could well be substantial audiences for schools, technical training, and rehabilitation programmes at other hours of the day. The likelihood is that a free-ranging service of complementary educational programmes would in time occupy the total capacity of the fourth channel, but if this proved not to be so, the spare capacity could either be given to an agency such as the NTF or hired out to the BBC or IBA, or other organisations who wished to make use of it. One obvious use is repeats of outstanding programmes, which at present crowd out original work. This support for an educational channel is given with the proviso that it should not lead to the transfer of all educational programmes to a ghetto channel or the isolation of educational broadcasting from contact with other broadcasting philosophies and styles.

The Commission's conclusions can be briefly summarised as follows:

i) The allocation of the fourth channel should not be made in haste.
ii) Before it is allocated, if it is to be allocated at all, thoroughgoing research is needed into the various proposals for its use and their relationship to social needs.
iii) The Government should undertake or commission whatever research is necessary to determine social needs and the viability of schemes proposed to meet them.
iv) In the light of present evidence, a majority of our Commission supports a fourth channel devoted to national and regional specialist educational services.
v) A minority is in favour of allocation to the IBA, under strict conditions.

CABLEVISION

So far our Report has been concerned with the strengths and weaknesses of the existing broadcasting institutions and ways of improving their performance. But looking ahead over the next twenty years it is possible that technological developments, some already with us, others merely gleams on the horizon, will invite a radical constitutional change in the nature of the broadcasting system as we know it. As its effectiveness grows and costs go down, *satellite transmission* could conceivably by the late 1980s add four channels to the number on view nationally, but much development work remains to be done. It would, at least in prospect, increase the scope of international television broadcasting. A second development is *videotape* recorder-player and cassette, which enables the user either to record programmes off his television set, to make his own material, or to purchase cassettes of pre-recorded material and play them back off a conventional set. It is, in short, a visual equivalent of the familiar sound tape recorder and cassette, and provides the same flexibility. The equipment is already on the market, though the high cost of both recorders and cassettes is a deterrent to widespread use. The third development, still in its experimental stages but likely to be in production within two or three years, is a new system giving television viewers the choice of extra push-button information on their screens: the IBA's variant is called *ORACLE*, the BBC's *CEEFAX*. CEEFAX, for example, takes the form of a small box with a number of push-button keys which can be attached to a normal television set. Viewers could choose from thirty-two pages displayed on the screen at the press of a button. Each page would resemble a teleprinted message, carrying items like weather forecasts, news summaries, stock market prices, etc., and updated from minute to minute by fitting the 'pages' into the fifty 'gaps' which occur each second within the television signal. The fourth, and perhaps most important, development is *cablevision*, the transmission of radio and television services from a central source to receiving sets by means of wire instead of over the air. All these developments multiply the services which television can provide, and the first, second and fourth are all means of transmitting messages which can bypass broadcasting institutions as we know them. Patently, such a possibility raises large political and social questions. If foreign programmes can be received directly on household sets, if home or commercially produced programmes can be circulated, bought and sold, as easily as sound tapes, the system of licensing all radio and broadcasting sources under strict Government control would be under serious pressure, and if commercial cable companies were freely allowed to produce programmes as well as relay them, again the pressure on broadcasting institutions would be severe and their role within the total system of television communication substantially altered. It is not within our competence to deal with all these questions in the light of present evidence, but we think it worthwhile to make some observations on the development which is mounting the most immediate challenge to the broadcasting institutions – cablevision.

Already by 31 July 1973, 12·60 per cent of licence holders were receiving programmes through relayed wire services – 2·85 per cent from systems run from non-profit-making bodies, 9·75 per cent from systems run by commercial companies – both operating under licence from the Ministry of Posts and Telecommunications. The only companies allowed experimentally to *originate* programmes are those which are supplying programmes of local interest for a few hours a week in five areas – Bristol, Greenwich, Sheffield, Swindon and Wellingborough – to test systems and the market, before any widespread introduction of cable services in this country.

The advantage of cablevision is that a single cable can carry as many as sixty channels, along which can pass not only conventional television programmes but also information services of various kinds, from local shopping guides to educational material which can be tapped whenever the consumer desires. In Toronto one such channel is used to present computer analysis of stock exchange dealings, another for a community channel offering local shows and English lessons, another for an ethnic channel broadcasting in a different language each day of the week, another for classified advertisements. In Boulder, Colorado, one of thirty channels is used to link computers to talk directly to each other. Through cable, two-way communication is possible: emergency services, car-hire firms, shops, education facilities, can be contacted at the press of a button; and conversely local authorities can sound public opinion or television companies do instant market research through the use of this facility. These are not futuristic ideas, all of them are actually in operation in parts of Canada and the United States.*

On the other hand, there is evidence that United States cable companies which provide their own television programmes as an alternative to those of the networks, have made no great headway except when they have obtained a monopoly of such items as sporting events.

That many of these services would be socially useful is beyond question but how much would they cost? How long would it take to provide a nation-wide cable system? How important is such a communications system compared with the improvement of development of other social services? And who would control such a system? As to time, the Post Office said in a Press release of 23 February 1972:

> More than 6,000 new homes will be equipped by the Post Office during the next 12 months with twin-cable systems carrying telephone service and 'piped' radio and television programmes into the house. Although the cable systems, which are installed while the houses are being built, can be used immediately for telephone, television or radio service, they will play a key role in bringing into the home other services which could well revolutionise urban life by the turn of the century.

*Brenda Maddox, *A Multi-Channelled Future* (Symposium of Broadcasting, University of Manchester, 1973).

The Report of the Television Advisory Committee, 1972,* estimates a period of ten to thirty years, depending on the availability of capital, popular demand and government agreement. The cost of a national coverage wired distribution system would be £500 m. to £1,500 m. in capital expenditure, depending on the type of system and the number of programmes catered for. Both estimates, of time and cost, would appear to be optimistic if the Post Office is to meet its other priorities first. However, both over-air services and access schemes have been introduced first in urban areas, and the same strategy could be adopted for cable systems subject to the cautions mentioned below. Only a major political decision would make feasible the provision of a widespread cable system before the mid-1980s, and if provision only began at that date, it is unlikely that the system would be completed by the turn of the century. Any such political decision, we believe, should be preceded by an extensive and informed public debate, a Government Inquiry covering all the relevant social as well as technical questions, and more extensive experiments to determine the kind of cable systems best suited to the needs of this country, and all these as soon as possible.

As to the effects of cablevision on the broadcasting institutions, there is this to be said. Commercial cable companies would inevitably concentrate on the large urban centres of population. People living in rural areas or unable to afford to join the service would be excluded. If the cable companies could deny material to the existing broadcasting organisations, either by buying exclusive rights to particular events or signing exclusive contracts with performers, this would seriously reduce the number of people at present able to enjoy them. Similarly, if commercial companies became originators as well as relayers of programmes, the resulting competition with the broadcasting organisations would be inflationary. Another consideration is that even if these difficulties were overcome, organisations broadcasting over-air would still be needed by the increasing number of people who possess portable television receivers. But there are even larger issues than these. In a free society it seems a good thing to have as many sources of communication as possible. Biases, quality, standards of production can sort themselves out, and each individual choose whate'er he will. This, theoretically, is the situation with regard to the Press and publishing. But before jumping to the conclusion that many television sources, like many newspapers, are of benefit to the public, there are other factors worthy of regard. Already there is a tendency for the rising costs of advertising (and

*Papers of the Technical Sub-Committee, p. 81.

the advent of television 'commercials') to kill off newspapers and for those remaining to fall into fewer and fewer hands. Outright commercial competition does not necessarily make for a multiplicity of information sources, but can have the opposite effect. Since the costs of providing television programmes, certainly to the artistic and technical standard now familiar to the British public, are exceedingly high and continually rising, it is only too likely that a free-for-all among commercial companies would in fact lead to less choice, poorer quality, lack of invention and ultimately to control by those with the longest purse. First-class television services require a high degree of professional competence at every level. Producers and technicians need careful training; performers have to be brought on with similar care if they are to give of their best, even when they have great natural talent. Even if they flushed out people of talent in larger numbers than seems likely, it is doubtful if small organisations would train professional broadcasters and nurture performers to the present standards. Contrariwise, if organisations developed on a scale matching that of the BBC and IBA and able to provide programme material of similar variety, quality and scope, they could conceivably exert similar influence without present safeguards. Another argument in favour of national networks is that their productions provide the whole nation with at least some common ground. We believe this to be increasingly important in an age when knowledge grows more specialised, cultures and sub-cultures and value systems are so varied, the sheer volume of available information makes assimilation difficult, and sharp differences in personal experience make communication and understanding between people more difficult than it has ever been. In short, we believe that for the foreseeable future, certainly beyond the turn of the century, the special position of the existing broadcasting institutions must be protected and the greatest care should be taken over the licensing of new originators of programmes, not from any desire to curb freedom but to preserve it. In saying this we distinguish between commercial pressures that would reduce multiple sources to a drab uniform superficiality, and genuinely local, specialist and even eccentric sources. There can, we recognise, be a danger in the very professionalism of broadcasting stifling personal and communal communication.

Peering through a periscope at future horizons is always a risky operation. We make no large claims, therefore, for our speculations about the structure of British broadcasting at the turn of the century. All we can do for the present is mention one or two principles and some of the factors which we think should influence the shape of the future. The first principle is that before decisions are made the public should be drawn into a debate based on adequate information concerning all the possible options. At present, the public is not well informed, nor does it show much curiosity about the condition of broadcasting, and this apathy is shared by far too many politicians. The second principle is that radio and television should be assessed in relation to the communications needs of the country as a whole. The recommendations of the Select Committee Report, 25 and 29, support this view and we would draw attention to them:

> (25) The need for a consumer organisation, established by statute, for all communications media should be included in the Minister's deliberations on the future of television after 1976 (para. 91).
>
> (29) The Minister should set up a full ranging enquiry at the earliest opportunity to consider broadcasting after 1976. This enquiry should consider not only the BBC and the Authority, but also take into account newer technological developments. Such an enquiry should study the systems of other countries and commission studies of the long term social, cultural, economic, political and technical implications of alternative systems and invite public debate to consider the options open (para. 167). There should, thereafter, be periodic and systematic reviews of the operations of the chosen structure (para. 128) and of the new technological developments which are introduced (para. 136).*

The third principle is that the provision of broadcasting services should be governed by concern for programmes of high quality, and not by the desire to provide markets for 'hardware' manufacturers: i.e. what appears on the screen should remain the paramount concern, not the system of transmission. For this reason, despite the inevitable charge of supporting a restrictive practice and patently contradicting our own argument favouring variety of choice, we believe that strict control over the licensing of programme originators will continue to be necessary. At the national level, we believe that the provision of programmes should remain in the hands of the BBC and the IBA, perhaps fed to a greater extent by tributaries of independent productions and that broadcasting relay companies should be required to pay rentals for the right to carry BBC and IBA programmes. Cable companies should not be allowed to develop an

* *Second Report from the Select Committee on Nationalised Industries*, Session 1971–2, Independent Broadcasting Authority (formerly Independent Television Authority), HC 465.

alternative national network. If the position of the main broadcasting institutions were to be seriously undermined, we believe that professional standards, the quality of programmes and the range of categories of programmes would in all probability decline, and that even if there were greater variety in some respects, it would be within a narrower compass and of poorer quality. It is difficult, also, to see how broadcasting could continue to play its part in systematic mass education. The broadcasting institutions should in addition be strong enough to retain an interest, though not necessarily a dominant one, in the provision of local services, but at this level, once the necessary multi-channel cable systems exist, there is much to be said for variety and competition. On the face of it, cable television will play an important role in building up and providing a means of expression for local communities, but we suspect that the main value of cable will prove to be not the provision of conventional television programmes but the supplying of information services and an apparatus for public conversation. Whether and how a balance might be struck between the Ministry of Posts and Telecommunications, the broadcasting institutions and private commercial companies in the development and control of a cable system, we cannot at present determine, but simply note the problem, and recommend very careful preliminary inquiries on these matters, as well as the kind of system, or systems, best suited to this country. We do not foresee that satellite transmission will radically affect the broadcasting services before the turn of the century and therefore leave it out of account. Videotape cassettes could become a major influence but we suspect that just as radio has not been damaged by sound-recording apparatus, records and cassettes, neither will the television services be greatly affected by wider use of videotape. The likelihood is that a limited number of groups and individuals will use specialist interest videotape cassettes and that educational and public authorities will build up libraries of such cassettes which can be drawn upon at the user's convenience. Such libraries would be a very valuable educational instrument, substantially add to the variety of television material available, permit users to watch what they want to at the most convenient time, and give a permanent form to much valuable material that is at present transient. In conclusion, we would draw attention to the fact, obvious in itself but sometimes overlooked, that viewing of any kind is only part of life and that even with increased leisure time, people will only be able to employ a fraction of the available communications systems for a limited part of the day; the more sources of communication there are, and the more numerous the messages, the fewer will be the recipients of each. The nub of the matter is that the more closely the use of radio and television approximates to private conversation, the more this defeats the chief advantages of mass media which are to make private conversation and activity public.

3 ACCOUNTABILITY

Once the aims of broadcasting have been determined and suitable broadcasting structures created, the next question is: How can society keep its broadcasters up to the mark? Institutions and individual broadcasters alike can be regarded as 'gatekeepers' in the sense that they exercise editorial control over the selection, content and quality of whatever is transmitted. Those who make the countless daily choices which decide what subjects are to be treated, who is to appear, the style of treatment, the general balance of programmes and all the other thousand and one considerations, bear a heavy responsibility. However conscientiously they perform their duties (and in general it is right to say that there is a great sense of responsibility among those who work in broadcasting), since Parliament and the public have an obvious interest in what is broadcast, there is a need for mechanisms through which the broadcasters must, whenever necessary, give an account of their stewardship. This question of responsibility and accountability has reference to the relationship between the broadcasting institutions and Government, the broadcasting institutions and the general public, and the broadcasting administrations and their employees. It also involves broadcasting policy, matters of taste, questions of fairness and response to public needs.

Government is concerned with broadcasting because it allocates limited airspace, issues licences to broadcast, and must decide on and pursue whatever it judges to be in the national interest, no less in the matter of broadcasting than in any other. No government could tolerate a broadcasting service which was systematically trying to usurp its role or subvert its policies. Consequently, there are statutes and charters which define the role of organisations licensed to broadcast, prescribe their aims and lay down the conditions under which they operate. Under the Wireless Telegraphy Act of 1949, no one may establish or use any station, or apparatus for wireless telegraph, except under a licence granted by the Ministry of Posts and Telecommunications. In theory, the Minister could license anyone to set up a transmitting station to broadcast, but in practice, for reasons of policy, he does not. The main reason is that it would be wrong, in the general opinion, for the most persuasive and influential medium of communication to rest in the hands of those with the longest purse or under State control. Instead, broadcasting has been vested in the public corporation, and the custom of reaffirming the independence of the broadcasting authorities has established this as a doctrine possessing constitutional force; that is, it is well nigh impossible to envisage any circumstances in which a government would consider it proper and desirable to renounce the doctrine of broadcasting independence.

In brief, this doctrine is that in technical matters, the Minister has, and exercises, the power to regulate the activities of the broadcasting authorities in considerable detail: in the field of finance, the Government controls the BBC's income by prescribing the amount of the licence fee and, indirectly, Independent Television's finances through a levy on profits, and by requiring capital investment by the BBC and IBA (but not the private programme companies) to be included in the report on public expenditure annually submitted to Ministers through the Ministry, but the broadcasting authorities are independent in the day-to-day conduct of their affairs, including programme content. Apart from technical and financial control, the Government also has powers to appoint and dismiss Governors of the BBC and Members of the IBA, to veto programmes, and to require announcements to be broadcast.

All these powers are subjected to checks and balances. No government would wish to make the appointments of Governors and Members political because its own set of nominees would be swept out whenever the Opposition party came to power. In practice, Governors have been appointed to ensure that controversial issues are, as far as possible, treated impartially, and there have been no dismissals. Dismissals would in fact require the virtual unanimity of all the political parties and the general public that Governors or Members had performed their duties irresponsibly. As to control of revenue, which mainly affects the BBC, the check on a government using it to control programme content is liability to exposure and the public outcry that would follow. To quote the Memorandum submitted by the Post Office to the Estimates Committee in 1969:

> The licence fee system is regarded as containing its own financial discipline. Any significant increase in potential revenue can only derive from an increase in the fee: and the Corporation cannot expect increases too often. In effect the BBC have to persuade the Government that it would be right to ask viewers and listeners for any more. There is thus in the mind of the public, a direct relationship between the services provided by the BBC and the amount of the licence fee.

The power to veto programmes is balanced by the broadcasting authorities' express right to broadcast an announcement that the Government has vetoed a programme. The Government has in fact used its power to forbid the BBC to express the opinion of the Corporation on current affairs and matters of public policy: and to forbid the broadcasting of subliminal messages – both bans being incorporated in the Television Act constituting the IBA. The first of these is founded on the inseparability of independence and impartiality; the second on the need to protect the public against subconscious persuasion. Otherwise the Minister has little or no departmental interest in the content of programmes. As for Government announcements, these relate to routine departmental business, rarely, if ever, the subject of Ministerial direction, and both BBC and IBA have the express right to broadcast that they are issued under Government direction.

The BBC and the IBA do not answer to the Minister for their performance in the day-to-day conduct of their affairs, nor does the Minister answer to Parliament. In effect they report to Parliament by annually presenting to it, through the Minister, an account of their plans, finance and work. If these reports failed to deal with a matter which interested Parliament, the Minister would direct that it be included. Both authorities are also liable to examination by a select committee of the House of Commons. The BBC was examined by the Estimates Committee in 1969; the IBA by the Select Committee on Nationalised Industries in 1972 and 1973. Other and continuing means by which Parliament can exercise a check on broadcasting performance are Questions, Early Day Motions, Adjournment Debates and the occasional Full Dress Debate. Members may also speak on broadcasting when the Consolidated Fund Bill is debated. By asking the Minister questions addressed to the use of his powers, members are able to comment on the performance of the broadcasting authorities. If such questions touch on their independence, the Minister declines to intervene, but the Member will still have made his comment. Early Day Motions may express disquiet about a programme or class of programmes or more general dissatisfaction. These motions are not debated but if they are strongly supported by Members' signatures they alert the broadcasting authorities to the existence of a significant Parliamentary view. If a clear consensus in Parliament were developing, without the Authorities apparently recognising it, the Minister could bring this to the attention of the governing bodies and, if necessary, direct them to deal with the issue in their annual report, without contravening the principle of intervention. In Adjournment Debates the subject of the motion is discussed, and speeches made by Members are answered by the Minister. If the subject is one in which the Government does not intervene, the Minister would remind the House of the fact. He might add that the broadcasting authorities would take note of what had been said, or that he would draw the attention of their chairman to the debate (an example is the Adjournment Debate on television trials*). Full Dress debates have taken place on such subjects as the BBC plan called *Broadcasting in the 70's*,† which proposed important changes in the Corporation's services, and on Conservative policy for broadcasting.‡

Thus there are checks on the abuse by Government of its powers and checks also on the performance of the broadcasting authorities. And the delicate balance between the responsibility of Government and the responsibility of the broadcasting authorities is held by custom hallowed over the years, by various ways in which public opinion can express itself, especially through Parliament, and by the existence of a general public confidence that Government will not dictate to the broadcasting authorities, nor the broadcasting authorities abuse their independence. What it amounts to is that the relationship between Parliament and the broadcasting institutions is governed by an unwritten law, a clear understanding on both sides

* *Hansard*, cols 1370–6, 28 December 1969.
† Ibid., cols 1523–624, 22 July 1969.
‡ Ibid., cols 1496–626, 3 December 1969.

of where the limits of tolerance lie. In practice the independence of the broadcasting authorities has been demonstrated in times of serious conflict. The BBC was, for example, able to hold to a policy uncongenial to the Government during the General Strike in 1926, during the Suez Crisis in 1956, and in 1972 when it arranged and broadcast a debate on Ulster by various parties to the conflict, despite the express wish of the Home Secretary, Reginald Maudling, who feared it might inflame the situation.

Both the broadcasting authorities have said in evidence that they do not fear Government pressure or interference, nor foresee any change in their relationship with Government. Nor have we observed signs of any serious public disquiet concerning that relationship. On the other hand there is some indication that those who work within the broadcasting industry do in fact experience pressures which contravene the spirit, if not the letter, of the doctrine of independence, and which affect the content and presentation of programmes. On the other side, there are the politicians, both of left and right, who feel unfairly treated or misrepresented by the broadcasters. This scarcely amounts to more than a certain bickering and disturbance of sensibilities, but it has created some uncertainty and insecurity within the BBC, which appears to bear the brunt of any political pressure, partly because of its prestige as a national institution, partly because it is centrally administered and has a clear chain of command, partly because of its larger output of documentary and current affairs programmes. Most of this friction seems to date from 1964, and to stem from the personalities of the Government and broadcasting executives during the intervening years. Previous to that year, day-to-day business was dealt with by contact between, respectively, the Chief Assistant to the Director General of the BBC and the Chief Whips, more difficult business being referred up on both sides to the Director General and the Lord President of the (Privy) Council and in very rare instances to the Chairman and Prime Minister. This system, we believe, was, and is, a good one, allowing traffic to flow which was beneficial to both parties and to the public, and establishing confidence and mutual understanding. That it was ever interrupted is, we believe, regrettable. There is no legislating for qualities of personality but we believe in and strongly reaffirm the need for politicians to respect the independence of the broadcasters, even if this at times means exercising much patience, and that every care should be taken to ensure not only that the Chairman, Director General and Governors of the BBC are persons of ability but capable of working together in a spirit of mutual trust and support. Ideal mechanisms for governing the relationship between broadcasting institutions and Government cannot, in the nature of the case, exist. There will always be some friction and this can only be kept to a minimum by the men who actually operate the system being of a calibre which induces mutual respect and wins public confidence.

The relationship between the broadcasting authorities and the public requires that the public which pays for the broadcasting services, either directly through the licence fee or indirectly through monies spent on advertising but ultimately charged to the consumer, should be broadly satisfied with the service provided. Since 'good broadcasting' has never been equated in the United Kingdom with whatever will satisfy the greatest number of people at any given moment (though we do not wish to imply that any broadcasting which achieves this is necessarily bad), this requires that a balance be struck between the mass audience and minorities. Any individual may enjoy a play by Chekhov, *Match of the Day*, one of the *Master Class* programmes, and *Callan*. For the whole man to be satisfied, the interests he shares with a few people have to be catered for as well as those he shares with the many. In addition, intensity of enjoyment must be considered as well as its extension. Such a service requires compromise, for though any individual could imagine a service which would exactly suit his tastes, it is plainly impossible to suit all the people all the time, when channels and airspace are in short supply. But if it is impossible to cater for every taste, it is equally undesirable always and everywhere to suit the taste of the majority. Many people do not realise what they would like until they have had it placed before them, and a television service would not be performing its duty of enlarging experience and raising the level of awareness if it simply aimed at the lowest level of satisfaction. A good broadcasting diet will include plenty of cakes and ale, high and low comedy, romance, suspense, satire, drama of all kinds, variety programmes and panel-games that are simply fun; but it needs to contain a certain 'weight' too, if the diet is not to be unbalanced. The more serious problems of existence must find their regular place, not just in the margins of the service but at peak times, be entrusted to producers, presenters and interviewers with sufficient intellectual grip, and treated in an appropriate style. Superficial or frivolous treatment is as distasteful as spreading steak tartare with candy floss. All these factors have to be borne in mind by the broadcasting authorities in extending the range of choice and planning the content of programmes within the limits available to them.

We can find no substantial evidence of universal public discontent with present programmes. On the whole, most people seem happy with what they get and are not actively critical of the service as a whole or individual programmes within it. This seems to be more the result of general public apathy rather than the outstanding brilliance of the programmes, though it must in fairness be remarked that there are more radio and television programmes which a person of lively curiosity might ideally like to see and hear than he is ever likely to have time for. At the same time it is possible to argue that the broadcasting services do fail the public in specific ways even though it has no sense of being failed; and that because they are justified by some specialised training, knowledge or experience which they possess, those who so argue are not necessarily to be dismissed on the grounds that they arrogantly presume to know what is good for other people. There are, of course, other critics who possess no special qualifications. These, too, are naturally entitled to represent their views. Others again may express personal views while representing them as those of the entire general public, and in some circumstances these can be mischievous.

Both the BBC and IBA have statutory and voluntary mechanisms for monitoring the state of public opinion. Both are required to have General Advisory Councils, at present appointed by the institutions themselves. The BBC General Advisory Council was first set up in 1934 'to secure the constructive criticism and advice of representative men and women over the whole field of its activity and to use their influence in helping towards a further understanding of the BBC's problems and policy on the part of the general public'. The General Advisory Council meets quarterly, when it receives a summary of major points of public criticism and hears and discusses a paper on some aspect of broadcasting prepared by the BBC but requested by the General Advisory Council itself. (The Governors receive a similar summary of public reaction every four weeks.) In 1965 the General Advisory Council Business Committee was set up to frame the agenda, make changes in Council procedure, review the balance of interests and geographical affiliations among the members of the General Advisory Council, and, more recently, to prepare, jointly with the BBC, a Press statement summarising its discussions. The Council has also begun to issue papers for the general public like *Taste and Standards in BBC Programmes*.

The IBA's General Advisory Council was set up by the Authority at the beginning of 1964 under 9(i) of the Television Act: 'To keep under review the programmes of independent television and to make comments to the Authority thereon; to advise the Authority on the general pattern and content of programmes and to consider such other matters affecting the independent television service as may from time to time be referred to it by the Authority.' Its meetings are held quarterly. Its Chairman presents Reports of Council meetings to the Authority two weeks before the Authority's own meetings. A Steering Committee has recently been constituted to meet ad hoc to advise on topical issues, and the General Advisory Council is empowered to initiate research studies and to invite whomsoever it will to supply direct to the Council information relevant to its work. This last provision is an attempt to meet the criticism frequently made of the two General Advisory Councils, that their relationship with the Corporation on the one hand and the Authority on the other is too cosy. Within the past year both the BBC and IBA have begun to explore ways of making their advisory councils more representative of the public and more autonomous in the conduct of their business. In addition to these general councils, both authorities have a number of regional and specialist Advisory Committees, and the BBC has National Broadcasting Councils for Scotland and Wales. The IBA has a dozen or so committees advising on medical, religious, educational and other such matters and the BBC has fifty-five advising bodies (not all of them carrying equal weight) dealing with general programmes, specialised subjects such as agriculture, charities, education, religion and music, an Engineering Advisory Committee and a Committee on the Social Effects of Television – altogether a total of 850 individual men and women.

Besides these networks of Advisory Councils and Committees, the broadcasting authorities are in touch with public opinion through their Audience Research Departments, employing scientific sampling techniques, through daily correspondence and telephone calls from the public, monitoring and daily summaries of the Press, meetings and correspondence with Members of Parliament, lectures by senior executives of the broadcasting organisations to the outside public and the criticism they hear at such functions, and through the comments and criticism which all their employees pick up from their friends, families and neighbours. The BBC's Audience Research Department, for example, now has thirty-seven years' experience of sampling techniques determining the size of audience and degree of audience appreciation, and of market research of the public which composes its audience, the times at which it can view or listen, its general habits, likes and dislikes, and its ability to absorb broadcasting information. The BBC also receives over a thousand letters a day, centrally addressed (apart from letters addressed to individual contributors), which are summarised weekly and monthly. Altogether, these various sources of information provide a formidable store of facts and opinion influencing the provision of services. There is, however, no obligation on either broadcasting authority to accept advice and criticism from outside except in the degree that it judges acceptance to be in its own interest. And it is questionable whether the institutions have found a successful way of gathering the views of the inarticulate. Plainly a broadcasting authority cannot systematically ignore advice without running the danger of antagonising the very public opinion on whose confidence and good will it depends for survival; on the other hand it can be tempted at times to resist radical criticism (for institutional considerations) which might well be in the public interest. A second limitation is the fact that the bulk of institutionally directed research is bound to be more concerned with charting the public's present habits, tastes and opinions than with assessing longer-term trends and consequences or the application of these to practical policy whenever they are relevant.

The charges most commonly made against the broadcasting services by individuals and groups (sometimes in the name of the general public but without much supporting evidence) are these:

i) Too many programmes offend against accepted standards of manners and morals.
ii) Programming is excessively weighted in favour of entertainment.
iii) Programmes purporting to be serious trivialise and oversimplify complicated issues.
iv) Particular programmes distort facts and misrepresent opinions.
v) Emphasis on what is pictorially dramatic gives some events more significance than they deserve and in general creates a false perspective.
vi) The cumulative effect of many programmes is to promote false values and glamorise anti-social behaviour which the young are tempted to imitate.
vii) The hypnotic effect of television lures people away from more creative employments and impedes social conversation to the detriment of families and society.
viii) Television deals in half-truths, flatters the glib, demeans those in authority and leads to a kind of universal scepticism.

These charges seem to fall into three categories. There are those which concern matters of taste, social habit or custom and are usually provoked by bad language, explicit portrayal of sexual activity and styles of life that are unconventional. The second category has to do with the misrepresentation of facts and opinion and the unfair treatment of persons appearing on television and radio. The third category has to do with the social effects of radio and television.

We believe that the first category of complaints, those to do with taste and convention, although probably the most publicised, are the least in importance and the least capable of remedy. In British society today there are wide divergences of view as to what is and is not acceptable human behaviour and what should or should not be portrayed on the screen. Judgements in matters of taste are notoriously subjective and what is acceptable in such matters differs from one social group to another, one area of the country to another, and one generation to another. It is difficult to see how detailed ground rules could be formulated, even were they desirable, which would prevent any scene, word or reference that could conceivably give offence to an individual or social group from reaching the screen. There are, of course, limits to public tolerance – detailed portrayals of a public execution or a sexual assault on a child would arouse widespread revulsion – but generally speaking the broadcasting services keep well within these limits, have adequate guidelines for producers, and perhaps err excessively on the side of caution. It is true that certain programmes and scenes (e.g. the comedy series *Till Death Us Do Part* for its language or the drama series *Country Matters* for its nude scenes), have attracted criticism from the National Viewers and Listeners Association and attention in the Press, but we can find no evidence that these represent the true state of popular feeling and it would be a mistake to mollify a small minority simply because they speak loudly. A radio or television series which never gave offence, never challenged received ideas or social customs, which adopted the taste of one class or social grouping as its own, which shied away from the full variety of human behaviour, would be boring, anodyne and untruthful, and wasting its potential to broaden mental horizons and enlarge the sympathy between different social groups. At the same time people should not be forced to watch what they do not wish to watch, and the greatest safeguard in this respect is not some form of internal or external censorship but the provision of a wide range of choice, together with such existing common-sense regulations as that which places after 9 p.m. programmes unsuited to family viewing or calling for a more than normally sophisticated approach to the problems of living.

Misrepresentation of facts and opinions and unfair treatment of persons appearing on radio and television is a different issue, for here there is a reasonable chance of establishing the objective facts and making an objective judgement about them. People with specialist knowledge who believe that a programme has got its facts wrong, individuals or organisations who, like the TUC, feel that they are misrepresented or have their operations regularly shown in an unfavourable light, and those who feel that interviews and discussions are concerned with the wrong questions or the right questions in the wrong context, or proceed on wrong assumptions, should certainly have access to a complaints machinery which can remedy justified grievances. The issue is not a simple one, for even when the facts can be established beyond dispute, they may give rise to different interpretations or a sense of grievance which is no more than an unwillingness to accept differences of opinion. Certain kinds of programme are more likely than others to invite charges of unfairness: for example, the drama shading into documentary, and the documentary shading into current affairs. In such cases, the broadcasters have a special responsibility to label programmes so that the public knows exactly what it is getting, and can make due allowances. Normally, when the subject is a topical one and illustrative material is plentiful, the producer's own sense of responsibility to the subject and to his audience, and the BBC's recommended order of procedure – first, research; second, shoot; third, edit; fourth, commentary – are the best guarantees that a documentary will be respectful of the truth. The existence of living individuals in considerable numbers with first-hand experience of the subject is also a check of sorts on current affairs documentaries. Greater problems arise in the case of news items which sometimes have to be produced at great speed and under pressure, and historical documentaries. Programmes in this latter category have been severely criticised for their inaccuracies and evident bias and it is one in which special care is required. There may be few or no living survivors to correct a programme's version of events. A paucity of pictorial material may tempt the producer to cut his commentary to fit his pictures. Or, a producer interested in a particular subject, but ignorant of its more general historical background, may champion one view at the expense of others equally plausible, or, through ignorance of the historical context, adopt a theory outstanding more for its ingenuity than its veracity. Yet another temptation is to read contemporary views into the past or pick out what happens to be of interest at the present day. Historical programmes should aim to illustrate the past and increase understanding, not re-write it to support some contemporary attitude or theory, titillate the audience, or flatter its vanity by indulging feelings of superiority. In the actual making of such programmes, the ordinary method of procedure is not suitable. Professional historians of different viewpoints, where different viewpoints exist, should be invited to help with and approve the commentary before, and not after, the search for pictorial material, and there should be close consultation right up to the process of final editing. Such consultation would, we believe, have forestalled the charge that series of programmes like *The British Empire*, *The Edwardians*, *Who Sank the Lusitania?* and *The Great Boer War* were little better than *romans à thèse*. As for those who are very much alive and who complain about inaccurate programmes or unjust treatment, we believe, firstly, that complaints would be fewer if the broadcasting authorities made a greater effort to explain the practical mechanics of production, so raising the level of public understanding and inducing realistic expectations; and, secondly, in the development of a complaints machinery which would invite public confidence.

A narrow majority of our members believe that a small independent Complaints Committee would be seen to be the best answer. This, they think, should be set up and financed by the Government rather than the broadcasting authorities; former professional broadcasters should be among those appointed to it; it should deal with complaints against both broadcasting authorities, and its terms of reference be strictly limited to cases of inaccuracy and misrepresentation after, and only after, the complainant has not received satisfaction from the broadcasting authorities themselves. The broadcasting authorities should be obliged to broadcast their judgements on either radio or television, whichever is the cause of complaint, and those who seek redress should not have to waive their ordinary rights in law. Without implying criticism of the impartiality of those at present serving on the BBC Programmes Complaints Commission and the IBA Complaints Review Board, it does not seem satisfactory to these members that the broadcasting authorities should themselves appoint judges over contested matters. A substantial minority are, however, opposed to this scheme on the grounds that it would derogate from the ultimate responsibility of the Governors of the BBC and Members of the Authority, that it would little by little enlarge its sphere of interest, that to make fair judgements its members would have to get too close to the institutions, and that the Government is not the best agency for establishing such a judicial body. All our members are agreed in rejecting the idea of a Broadcasting Council with statutory powers to direct the BBC and IBA in other matters of programme content. The arguments against a Broadcasting Council supervising and regulating every aspect of broadcasting are these: such a council would undermine the wise principle enunciated in the Pilkington Report that authority and responsibility for the exercise of authority should go together. If it became, as it inevitably would, concerned with the day-to-day production and content of programmes, this would fudge the present clear line of responsibility leading up to the Governors of the BBC and the Members of the IBA Authority, and if it became ultimately responsible for programmes itself, the quality of its members, and especially of their practical judgement, would become just as crucial as that of the present Board of Governors or Members of the Authority. There would simply be the added difficulty of deciding who would constitute the Council, its responsibilities, terms of reference, methods of working, and to whom it should be answerable. It is also difficult to envisage how such an overseeing body could manage a truly competitive system, which in the nature of the case requires that each broadcasting authority should be kept to some extent in the dark about the detailed plans of its rival. We believe that in practice such a Broadcasting Council would be unworkable, demoralise programme makers, who would, more than ever, be looking over their shoulders, and lead to less rather than more varied and imaginative production. And, in general, we are inclined to think that failings, often traceable to personal temperament, cannot be remedied simply by fiddling about with structures. Our own positive proposal for reinforcing the structures of British broadcasting will be found in a later section of our Report.

The third category of complaints is at once the most important and the hardest to verify. It concerns the social effects of radio and television. Anthony Wedgwood Benn, in his speech at the 1972 Manchester Symposium, 'External Influences in Broadcasting', summarised the problem thus: 'Similarly the anxieties being expressed worldwide about the effects of violence and sex on television as a corrupting force undermining the traditional role of the educational system in preserving cohesive social values within society indicates a growing suspicion that the influence of television may be greater than the influence of schools in shaping the whole character of our people.' Milton Shulman, perhaps the critic most consistently disturbed by the potential influence of the medium, describes television as: 'A ravenous eye subtly playing on values, surreptitiously absorbing institutions, steadily shifting foundations and traditions.'* Professional broadcasters themselves have admitted to

**The Ravenous Eye* (Cassell), p. 8.

anxieties on this score. In a television interview in December 1972, David Attenborough, formerly the Director of Programmes, BBC Television, said: 'One of the things that worries me, which you can't very well say if you're a Director of Programmes, is that people watch television too much. The average man spends more time watching television than any other activity except his work and sleeping.' Television has been blamed for a wide variety of social phenomena, the escalation of violence, the hippy movement and its rejection of conventional mores and standards, the revolt against parental and institutional authority, the rise in drug taking, poorer reading standards, and so forth. More broadly, television is accused of promoting anti-social values. To quote Milton Shulman again:

> Only a tiny segment of television encourages the young to be socially aware, to be co-operative and responsible, to be community conscious, to value the truth, to despise cruelty, to cultivate a sense of duty, to be charitable, to be selfless, to be kind. Most of it is indifferent or neutral about social values, inculcates little sense of communal duty or responsibility, promotes the acquisition of goods as a criterion of success, glamorises the trivial and superficial, justifies violence as a means to moral and legal ends, encourages an escapist approach to reality and concern, builds up false expectations, stimulates an undue craving for material rewards. Broadcasters do not transmit these values deliberately or callously; they are the accidental by-products of the system.

This kind of moral censure, not of individual programmes but of the whole broadcasting system, generates powerful emotional support and opposition. Some will say that television itself has become a drug which leaves people uninvolved spectators of life at the expense of more life-enhancing activity: others that it brings enrichment to lives which in any case would be futile and empty. Some believe that television has a powerful influence on social values and behaviour, others that it simply reflects society, and that society itself must adopt different values before television can become a greater force for good. Some believe that television is a stronger influence on the young than home, school or church; others that these traditional tutors still effectively counterbalance the influence of television or that the influence of peer groups is more crucial than any of them. Some believe with Milton Shulman that television is impregnated with anti-social values, others that it encourages people to be kindlier, more tolerant, better informed, and more understanding. Some believe it persuades people to accept deviant behaviour as normal, others that by exposing and analysing such behaviour, it helps people to treat the deviant with greater compassion and enlightened common sense.

Many of these disputes arise from conflicting personal impressions. Many of the formulations involved are also at fault for suggesting that where mass communication exerts an influence, it typically does so indiscriminately and on a massive scale, falling, as it were, with equal impact on the just and the unjust alike. Though evidence on these matters is hard to come by, one conclusion that may safely be drawn from the body of existing research is that broadcast content will often affect different people in different ways, depending partly on the variety of other circumstances in which they are placed. Nevertheless, avoiding facile generalisations, society must be seriously concerned to determine the social effects of television, and we believe, therefore, that there is an evident need for systematic, prolonged and intensive research, to which Government, the broadcasting authorities, and all who are concerned with the well-being of society, should be parties. We think it unlikely that such research would confirm the worst fears of television's critics, i.e. that a vicious, violent and irrational generation is being bred solely or mainly by television. But the possibility cannot be dismissed out of hand, and the quicker there are facts to go on, the quicker can any harmful effects of television be remedied. Meanwhile we believe the broadcasting authorities should be especially sensitive to the possibility that television cumulatively affects the attitudes of at least significant numbers of people to three subjects in particular; violence, acquisitiveness and truth. There is a plausible case to be made that the cumulative effect of many programmes, especially imported films and crime serials, is to reinforce the idea that human development and happiness can be identified with the acquisition of material goods, to gain acceptance for the notion that it is justifiable to use violence so long as the cause is good, and to diminish awareness that the pursuit of any truth requires continuous and painstaking effort. This is not to say that television should portray only characters brimming over with the finest human qualities but that popular entertainment should beware of creating stereotypes which project false values and which the young especially may be tempted to adopt as models for imitation.

In saying this, we recognise that broadcasting institutions and those who work in them are subject to the usual human failings and will always fall short of absolute ideals. We realise that producers cannot be continuously concerned with ultimate values. Their problems are often more mundane, especially if they are working under pressure: which participants to invite, where and what to film and transmit, how to keep within a budget, getting the script right, coaxing people of different temperaments to work in harmony. Structures can, and should, be designed to make the producers' task easier, but they cannot replace the producer's chief assets – the eye, the heart, and the imagination. The sudden flash of illumination, spontaneous inspiration, lightning stroke of imagination which raise a programme above the level of the commonplace, cannot be guaranteed or planned for in advance. And just as small rubs of the green – a domestic quarrel, a headache, the state of the weather – affect the receptivity of the viewer and listener, so they can disturb the creative mood of the producer. All this has to be taken into account, but it is still true that values consistently reflected on and encouraged by the institutions, and which have entered the bloodstream of those engaged in production, will subtly affect even routine decisions and choices.

So far we have not touched on the broadcasting authorities' public relations and consultations with the public on policy matters. It has frequently been said that both broadcasting authorities are opaque, defensive and unwilling to consult with the public before adopting policies which affect the service provided. Without going into the rights and wrongs of particular instances, we would say that it is in the interests of the broadcasting authorities themselves, as well as of the public, that the operations of the broadcasting institutions should be as open as possible to public scrutiny, and that advice and information should flow freely between the authorities and the public. In the past, both the BBC and IBA have given needless offence by springing changes in policy on the public without prior public debate. The BBC has since admitted that it would have been wiser to make known its thoughts and invite criticism before launching its policy document, *Broadcasting in the 70's*. Similarly, the IBA would have been well advised to reveal its mind well before setting out its detailed claim to the fourth channel, or adjusting the regional boundaries of transmission between Yorkshire and Anglia Television. We accept that competitive services must preserve some degree of secrecy concerning their future programmes, but this argument does not hold with regard to major policy changes. Indeed the authorities would have much to gain from taking the public into their confidence, not only by profiting from ideas and suggestions received from outside, but because their policies are often based on information they have gathered through their research departments, information which is not generally available and frequently contradicts popular assumptions: to make it available at the earliest possible moment would do the authorities credit and forestall heated criticism based on inadequate information. It is to be hoped that present plans which enable the BBC's General Advisory Council to nominate half its members after consultation with outside bodies representing a substantial section of the public will be a step towards widening the area of consultation and establishing a more trustful relationship between the Corporation and the public. It would also, we believe, be in the public interest if, when the IBA is in process of granting franchises, the hearings were in public, and the Authority published its reasons for granting each franchise. Page 386 of Appendix 20 to the Report of the Select Committee on Nationalised Industries 1972, concerning the Canadian method of granting franchises, is a sufficient answer to those who feel that public hearings would inevitably be unfair to the companies. Finally, although we realise that both human and material resources are limited, we believe that both broadcasting authorities, in some instances through joint action, could make greater positive efforts to familiarise the public with their aims, structures, the ways in which programmes are made and the factors influencing them, the results of research, and the technicalities of transmission. Public ignorance and apathy are great. Publications on aspects of broadcasting are often excellent, but do not reach the wider public. A travelling exhibition or permanent exhibition (on the lines of the Independent Television Gallery in Brompton Road) in major city centres might help this process of public education. So, too, would occasional programmes about the broadcasting services themselves, perhaps made by independent producers to counter any suspicion of self-interested propaganda. The BBC's 50th Anniversary exhibitions and recent BBC programmes on the making of television news and the future of television were sporadic efforts of a kind we would like to see more regularly attempted.

Another variety of consultation, related to the broadcasting authorities' understanding of their duties, and their functions as servants of the public, is consultation over important social issues. If radio and television have a part to play in the creation of informed and socially just social policies, it is desirable that future Government decisions should be thoroughly aired in good time to enable the public to absorb the necessary information and make a judgement upon it. In practice, the broadcasting authorities sometimes treat such issues too late in the day, even when their importance has been drawn to their attention, or treat them as news items instead of ongoing concerns requiring continual attention in the interest of public participation. One such instance was the reorganisation of the National Health Service. The main lines of Government thinking were given in a consultative document issued in May 1971. The White Paper was published in August 1972 and a book on proposed management arrangements in September 1972. Up to the end of February 1973, no major BBC or IBA television programme had focused on the central issues of this reorganisation – this despite the fact that the proposed changes were severely criticised in professional journals, the national Press and at three national conferences in the summer of 1972. Such a delayed response seems to us a dereliction of duty on the part of the broadcasting services. If, as seems to be the case, the television services are for a majority of people their chief and most trusted source of information, and if it is accepted that in a participatory democracy the public have the right to express their views on the social services which intimately affect their daily lives, it is clearly necessary for the television authorities to provide information and facilities for discussion before the Government has committed itself. If the necessary information and discussion are forced to wait upon some relevant news item, the effect of public opinion on Government policies is diminished or nullified. In view of their evident responsibility in such matters, we believe that both broadcasting authorities should have some machinery for registering issues of national importance well in advance and ensuring that they are given adequate coverage. They should not be left entirely to the perspicuity and personal interest of individual programme makers.

The third relationship we wish to consider under the heading of accountability is that between the broadcasting authorities and those who are involved on both the artistic and the technical side in the making of programmes. In this instance we will confine ourselves to questions of principle. The first is that in today's society there is a growing sense that people should have a greater say in decisions which affect their own lives and working conditions. We believe that broadcasting institutions, not less than other industries, will have to take account of this in their procedures for formulating policy. The second principle is that valuable knowledge and experience which could contribute to better programmes should not be wasted. The more extreme suggestion favouring worker control, or the election of executives such as Heads of Department by all those working within a particular department, could not logically be adopted in broadcasting where the customer, or audience, has no immediate means of redress; at any rate not before such participative arrangements are more widely used in society, for example in normal competitive business enterprise where the customer has more immediate protection in competition. But there should be full consultative structures at least equal to those used in the most progressive organisations.

Underlying this discussion of accountability is our concern that due respect should be paid to all the people who constitute the broadcasting audience, and who, no matter what the temptation, should never be manipulated, cheated, patronised or sold short. The best possible balance should be struck between their various, and often conflicting, needs and desires. Concern, too, that the institutions should have complete freedom from outside coercion to pursue the aims of good broadcasting, and that those with ultimate responsibility should have the power to conduct their business with these aims in view, and be both clearly identifiable and genuinely accountable. Mutual confidence and respect, and a free flow of information between the public and the institutions, are necessary conditions of a broadcasting system which will render the best service to all.

In the course of our study of the values and structures of broadcasting in Great Britain, and the questions of accountability, certain institutional inadequacies will have become apparent. The most striking of these is a lack of disinterestedness within the broadcasting institutions themselves, Parliament, whose interest in broadcasting is mainly political, and the appropriate unions, chiefly concerned with opportunities and conditions of employment. Secondly, there is the lack of a forum in which all those concerned about broadcasting can meet, and their voices be heard. Thirdly, there is no continuous review of broadcasting policy and developments; inquiries such as those headed by Beveridge and Pilkington have been invaluable and influential, but sporadic. Finally, the need for more research in depth, coordination of existing research by the broadcasting institutions and various university centres, and its application where appropriate to broadcasting practice, is recognised on every side. It is with these considerations in mind that we now wish to outline our proposal for a Centre for Broadcasting through which these deficiencies could be made good.

THE CENTRE FOR BROADCASTING

We have come to the conclusion that there is a place for a new body, independent of the present broadcasting institutions, whose chief task would be to consider, not occasionally, but continously, the art, philosophy, content and practice of broadcasting. This organisation, which we provisionally call *The Centre for Broadcasting*, could answer several present and future needs. There is the need of a meeting ground for Government and Parliament, broadcasting practitioners working both inside and outside the present institutions, and the general public; of a forum for all those who work within the broadcasting industry in whatever capacity; of a continuing dialogue between all those who have an interest in the broadcasting services on current needs and issues to which those responsible for the day-to-day running of services cannot always adequately attend; of a body capable of undertaking tasks which lie outside the limit of the existing institutions or could not be undertaken by them without inviting charges of institutional bias; a body through which popular needs and opinions could be expressed, but which would not usurp the responsibilities of those charged with the day-to-day provision of services; a body continuously reflecting on overall broadcasting policy and able to initiate, and act as a clearing house for, research into particular aspects of broadcasting; a body to which Government could turn for reliable advice based on objective evidence, and which could act as a stimulus to the broadcasting institutions and undertake public education on broadcasting matters. We believe that such a body, occupying the middle ground between Government and the broadcasting institutions, would be of benefit to both.

The Centre for Broadcasting would need to fulfil the following requirements:

i) It must be designed to exclude meddling in the detailed administration of the broadcasting organisations. The intention would not be to create a broadcasting overlord or back-seat driver, such as a Broadcasting Council. It would be concerned with questions of overall policy, research, the provision of information and advice, and serve to make known minority views to broadcasting services.

ii) Its membership will need to include representatives (not only of managerial and administrative rank) of the broadcasting institutions and other people with a detailed knowledge of their workings.

iii) Its membership and activities should reflect public opinion as a whole, insofar as this can be ascertained, and it must be capable of promoting informed public debate. It must possess an executive arm capable of undertaking whatever tasks its governing body resolves upon, or has had entrusted to it.

iv) It must possess the necessary authority to ensure that it is in fact consulted by those it exists to serve, and that its recommendations be taken seriously.

v) It must be financially viable.

The purpose of the Centre can be summarised as follows:

i) To keep under constant review the art, philosophy, content and practice of broadcasting, having particular regard to its social effects.

ii) To promote informed understanding between the broadcasting organisations and the community at large.

iii) To ensure that account is taken of the extent and nature of the expansion of public demand on the communications media in general and upon broadcasting in particular.

iv) To promote public understanding and debate of any issue concerned with the broadcasting services.

v) To undertake, promote, or co-ordinate, at the request of Government, the broadcasting organisations or other clients, research into particular aspects of broadcasting.

Control would be vested in a Council. The formula for appointment would run as follows: 'Members would be nominated by the interests they represent and appointed by the Minister of Posts and Telecommunications.' Membership would include representatives of local and regional authorities; national social welfare and cultural organisations; educational bodies; the churches; the trade unions and industry; government and the broadcasting institutions; and representatives from nine regional committees whose membership would roughly reflect that of the Council itself; all of these to serve on a triennial basis. The council would also form, at its own invitation, specialist panels of not more than six members each to provide a professional commentary on those matters affecting broadcasting which touch upon community and social affairs, the arts, the sciences, the technical sphere of transmission, formal and adult education, and entertainment.

The Centre's Secretariat would initially be made up of a permanent Director, appointed by the Council, chosen for his personal standing among those in the broadcasting industry, and paid at an appropriate level. In addition there would be six second-tier staff from the fields of interest covered by the specialist panels, a research and survey team of four members, and executive and clerical staff. The Secretariat would service both the Council and the regional committees and would be enlarged, in the light of experience, at the discretion of the Director.

The Centre's method of work would be:

i) To identify issues of public concern and to assess in dialogue with the BBC and IBA the extent to which account of them has already been taken in the formulation of broadcasting policies.
ii) To provide studies for the advancement of arguments in specific matters in which the Centre's Council felt that the response to the Corporation and the Authority should be further explored.
iii) To provide, upon consultation, advice concerning major formulations of new policy by central government or by the BBC and IBA individually.
iv) To advise upon the balance of coverage provided by broadcasting, within the communications media overall, of matters affecting regional life.
v) To keep under review technical developments and programme ideas overseas and bring to the attention of the broadcasting organisations those which seem worthy of adoption in this country.
vi) To provide on a generous scale popular information and academic studies on broadcasting matters, by publications and other means.

The estimated basic running costs of the Centre would begin at £250,000 rising to £1 m., this money to be provided by a government grant in aid established as a percentage of the levy, a levy on local authorities (on a capitation basis under S. 137 of the Local Government Act of 1972) and funds from private sources which the Council would be free to solicit.

The above account is no more than the bare bones of the Centre we envisage, and we have deliberately left the fine details for further consideration, e.g. the balance of representation, the financing, and the Centre's precise status. But we believe that the proposal is sufficiently worked out to make it both attractive and desirable, and that it contains the possibility of serving as a focus for all with specialist knowledge or particular interests relevant to broadcasting, and of servicing intelligent public debate. This seems more than ever necessary in the light of social changes and technical developments. It must be emphasised that it is not a Broadcasting Council in that it is not a broadcasting overlord, and differs from the National

Television Foundation in that it has no responsibility for providing broadcasting services, but we are convinced that such a body could provide an effective means of remedying the deficiencies we note in the broadcasting structures existing at present. We recognise, however, that no matter what its theoretical constitution or status, it would stand or fall by the quality of its membership, especially of its Director and Secretariat, and the quality of its work.

4 BROADCASTING AND EDUCATION

Broadcasting educates in two ways: through the general programme output, and through the systematic teaching of particular subjects and skills. The first way is usually referred to as 'educative' broadcasting, the second as 'educational' broadcasting. In this section of our Report we wish to discuss the specifically educational programmes for schools and for adults provided by both the BBC and the independent programme companies. We consider, however, that they should be seen in relation to the wider background. All broadcasting is in some sense a form of education; even the most pedestrian entertainment may provide some scrap of new knowledge or make some faint impression upon attitudes and values. For that reason the BBC has always maintained before successive Committees of Inquiry that its educational obligations under the Charter are and should be discharged primarily through the quality and impact of the whole range of its programmes. We endorse this view of the responsibilities of the broadcasting authorities, and believe that they are greatest towards that large section of the population for whom broadcasting is the principal avenue towards a greater understanding of the contemporary world, an enhanced appreciation of the arts of music and drama, and a wider acquaintance with men and women from many walks of life. Educative broadcasting is described by John

Scupham in his book, *Broadcasting and the Community*, as: 'The maintenance, extension and transmission of a culture.' This supposes that there are certain arts and skills, bodies of knowledge, codes of behaviour and shared values which make up a social heritage and must be handed on if society is to preserve its coherence and identity. It supposes too that there is a good, a better and a best, as well as a worse and plain bad in every aspect of life. It is often argued that the proper task of a broadcasting service is simply to give people what they want, and not to impose the value judgements of those in charge of it. We have dealt earlier in this Report with the fallacy of supposing the ratings are a true measure even of actual public demand, since the mass audience is an aggregate of minorities, each with its special tastes and interests. Still less do they measure potential demand. To accept fashion and the prevalent popular taste as the only criteria is to exclude any possibility of widening the range of peoples' sensibilities and enjoyments. We therefore believe unhesitatingly in the importance of a steady and deliberate effort to raise standards of taste, appreciation and discrimination in art, music, literature and the like, believing also that this implies value judgements beyond simply saying that something is good of its kind. Certainly a broadcasting service must present creative work of all kinds and to suit all tastes, but there is a world of difference between finding room for both Beethoven's Ninth Symphony and the latest pop tune, and presenting them in such a way as to suggest that they are really as good as each other, only different. Governments everywhere are committed to raising standards of taste, discrimination and judgement. The effort of the whole educational system is in that direction. It is reinforced by the public provision of libraries, art galleries and museums, and by Government support for the performing arts. Broadcasting institutions as public servants are especially effective instruments for the pursuit of the same end. Three-quarters of the adult population of the United Kingdom left school at the age of fifteen or earlier. For some of them the hazards of education and circumstance have sharply limited the range of broadcast programmes to which they are likely to respond. For many others, broadcasting is a readier way to understanding than the printed word.

There are no grounds for assuming that large numbers of people are born incapable of appreciating anything but undemanding entertainment, and abundant evidence that mass education has strikingly increased and is still increasing the numbers with the desire and ability to appreciate what is best. In 1961, Dr Joseph

Trenaman published a thesis which revealed that in 1957, 45 per cent of the population were resistant to new ideas and higher values; some 10 per cent were willing to grapple with the abstract and the intellectually complex; a further 25 per cent were prepared in spite of limitations of background and vocabulary to accept the presentation of serious material in a serious way; and yet another 20 per cent, of modest educational backgrounds, were willing to give their attention to similar material if it was presented in terms that were simple enough and seemed relevant to their lives.* This 'serious' audience has almost certainly grown beyond 55 per cent since 1957. 'Do not put upon the plate of Demos what you would not put upon your own' has always been a sound principle. Today Demos is increasingly likely to recognise insubstantial food if it is set before him. What he needs is good substantial food but cooked to suit his taste, and gradual familiarisation with new tastes and flavours.

There is, of course, every reason for broadcasters to proceed, like good teachers, from the known to the unknown; that is, to move outwards to new experience and information from what is already familiar to the learner. It is also part of a comprehensive broadcasting service to provide a full range of creative work, even the relatively trivial and ephemeral, and to suit the tastes of those who are 'resistant to new ideas and high values'; but the service as a whole should be provided in the awareness that it is indulging an imperfection in its audience, and be discouraged from becoming its accomplice.

However, we recognise that the definition of educative broadcasting as 'the maintenance, extension and transmission of a culture' may itself need expansion, given the nature of contemporary British society. There must be room for new voices. Old but unfamiliar cultures, and new sub-cultures, must be explored, interpreted and introduced to each other. As the various parts of the world grow increasingly inter-dependent, it becomes more important to have working knowledge of cultures which were once remote but now bear directly on our society. Buddhism, Hinduism and Islam are the native cultures of substantial portions of contemporary British society and they need comprehending, not only to increase international understanding but to develop harmony between fellow citizens in the United Kingdom itself. From being keepers of the national heritage, its art, architecture, literature, drama, music, religions and philosophies, those who work in broadcasting now must undertake a new role as teachers and interpreters of mankind's total inheritance. If this work is sensitively done, it will, we believe, highlight and

*John Scupham, *Broadcasting and the Community* (Watts), p. 85.

reinforce the criteria of what is best, by which the quality of all creative work and new ideas has to be judged.

Because the educational function of increasing knowledge, training minds, refining tastes, is so important and requires steady effort over a broad front, we are strongly opposed to shifting educative broadcasting onto a single wavelength or channel. The broadcasting services should be of such a kind that people are drawn, sometimes by accident, to hear and view what is unfamiliar and perhaps demanding. This has generally, though intermittently, been the practice of the broadcasting services, but we understand that economic and other pressures tend to undermine it. We believe that the broadcasting authorities should hold resolutely to the principle of mixed programming, and in no way contribute to the feeling among some producers of educational programmes that they are regarded as second-class citizens, whose activities get in the way of the real business of broadcasting, i.e. entertainment. Although we understand the reasoning behind the BBC's changeover from mixed programming on radio to 'streamed networks', we are inclined to think that the general reluctance to switch from one network to another locks listeners into voluntary mental ghettos, and forestalls the process of leading taste and widening horizons. Radio 1, especially, though indubitably popular, is almost totally undemanding and unchallenging. The fact that it is patronised so extensively by the young, does suggest that careful consideration should be given to how this audience, without being put to flight, could be given something to test its digestion. For much the same reason, it is regrettable if, during the critical peak viewing hours, the proportion of serious material is squeezed off the television screen, or, if the word 'serious' is redefined, to save the appearances but in reality narrow the range of what is on offer. The broadcasting services as a whole provide considerable variety and as much mental stimulation as any reasonable person could demand, but, as far as we can judge, too little of it finds its way onto the screen between 7 p.m. and 10 p.m. Once again we are faced with the odd fact that arguments about the 'broadcasting services' come down to the use made of the nine hours' peak viewing time on the three available television channels. Too much has to be crammed into that relatively short period of time.

Educational broadcasting covers radio and television for Schools, Further Education and the Open University. In all three areas, the main problems are lack of airspace or shortage of money.

The schools broadcasting services are extensive and of high quality. Their aim is to provide experience to children within the classroom which is not easily available from other sources; to exemplify the most up-to-date ideas on the curriculum and teaching methods; and to provide resources for both teachers and children. The services aim to be teaching aids, not a substitute for the living presence of a teacher, and increasingly they are designed to promote active participation on the part of the children. Practically all schools have equipment for radio reception, and 85 per cent equipment for television reception. In the year 1972/3, 32,000 used radio programmes, 25,000 television programmes, besides tape recordings, off-air videotapes, and television programmes available on film from the BBC. The BBC produces 120 separate series, 91 of them for the whole United Kingdom. Most of its radio series are broadcast in weekly instalments and cover three terms; 19 of its 29 television series are broadcast in fortnightly instalments. The BBC sends out free to all schools in the United Kingdom, six months in advance of each school year, annual programmes documents for Primary and Secondary Schools to help teachers plan the use of their broadcasts. Many programmes are reinforced by teachers' notes, pamphlets, kits, worksheets and work books, film strips, film loops, wall pictures, long-playing records, tapes and even hymn books. These productions have more than once broken new ground in the educational field and been imitated by other educational publishers. The BBC's schools broadcasting service has been operating for forty-eight years and its policy is determined by the Schools Broadcasting Council, an autonomous body of educationists, covering teachers' associations, local authorities, the Department of Education and Science and other educational organisations. The Council has Programme Committees to review needs and results, and Education Officers for day-to-day contact with the schools. Education is one field in which the BBC and IBA do not compete, but operate complementary services. Independent Television has been providing a schools service for fifteen years. Each programme company is required to present a minimum of nine hours of schools broadcasting per week in the academic year. The main networked programmes are produced by ATV, Granada, Thames and Yorkshire Television, but regional companies may vary the pattern or add local programmes, some of which may later be fully or partly networked. There are about twenty-six fully networked series each year. The IBA is advised by its Educational Advisory Council and its two committees, the Adult Education Committee and the Schools Committee, and the companies which regularly produce programmes also have their own Advisory Committees and Education Officers. The IBA issues about two hundred schools publications, provides a number of fellowships for teachers and lecturers for research into schools television, and is cooperating with the BBC and its Schools Broadcasting Council on a nation-wide project to show what can be achieved when a planned approach to curricula goals deliberately includes broadcasting, and is not frustrated by lack of equipment; some eighty schools have been selected as model case studies.

Although additional airtime is desirable, and could be profitably utilised, this is not the main problem for the schools broadcasting services. By far the greatest difficulty, at least for the BBC, is to find the necessary money. Schools pay a quarter of a million pounds in licence fees, but the BBC allocates 5 per cent (£5,751,000) of its income to educational broadcasting, which means that it is virtually subsidising the educational system. There seems to be a strong case in this instance for supporting the schools broadcasting through Government subvention if some means can be found to guarantee the independence of the education and broadcasting professions, and to stabilise income—though we appreciate that this involves choices between social services and also between various demands on the public monies made available for education. We believe that the conditions under which the Open University operates could be a useful guide to the development of the schools broadcasting services, and that the development of the best possible service is of the highest national importance. The educational and social ambience of children growing up between now and the turn of the century will become increasingly complex; technology is likely to bring about further dramatic changes in our way of life. Television will continue to be a major instrument for disseminating ideas and information about the surrounding world and teachers are almost certain to find that constructive use of a medium so built into the life of the community and their pupils is essential if they are to do their job properly. The quality and range of the schools broadcasting services (in conjunction with other educational services which we discuss below) will have a growing influence on the development and quality of our society as a whole. It seems to us that the time has now come for the establishment of a new agency, in which the government educationalists and the broadcasting authorities will be represented, to coordinate and supervise the whole range of broadcasting services. The Schools Broadcasting Council is itself an example of an accommodation between the various interests which can provide a pattern for the future. Through such an agency the government could channel funds and represent its views, the broadcasting authorities lend their expertise, and the educational organisations ensure that the service develops to meet new needs and in line with the best contemporary educational theory and practice. The agency would use funds from the Department of Education and Science to commission and buy in material from any source. Such a scheme, of course, would only work if the fourth channel were given over primarily to educational use, and a radio channel, if in a few years' time this becomes feasible, be similarly made available. These would carry the bulk of specialist educational services, but it would not be the intention to take all educational programmes off the general channels.

Turning from the supply of broadcasting services to their reception, we would observe that a schools broadcasting service cannot be effective unless receiving equipment is adequate, teachers are trained in the best use of both equipment and programmes, and children also know how to utilise the broadcast material to the best advantage. The willingness of Local Education Authorities to provide equipment for reception varies considerably: the charge upon their limited resources is certainly a heavy one but we believe that television can supply such teaching enrichment and is so economical of teaching resources as a whole, that the provision of equipment should have a high priority. The ideal would be for every school to have radio and colour television sets, and two sets of videotape and sound recording equipment, projectors and a library of videotape cassettes, properly serviced and administered by a communications officer. This provision is, of course, dependent on the Government's, and the nation's, willingness to invest in education, but it is also, to some extent, linked with the desire and willingness of teachers to incorporate broadcast material into their teaching practice. There is some evidence that many teachers still regard broadcasts as a diversion or distraction from 'real' teaching and that others who have no objection in principle feel technically incompetent or unsure how to make best use of broadcasts. Many schools are now helped by media resources officers in charge of a media resources centre, and teacher training is now available in many colleges of education, university departments and through in-service training. Twelve university centres and thirty-four colleges of education already have the equipment to make audio-visual material. All this will in time improve teachers' facility in employing audio-visual material, and research being conducted by the IBA, involving 100 schools in 57 local education authorities, into the use of educational programmes, will also improve the effectiveness of schools broadcasting. Recording and storage facilities for material taken off-air will also enable teachers to make more convenient use of broadcasts, though, especially in science subjects, there is a danger of using recorded material which is out of date, out of context, or out of order, and copyright regulations may need extension and modification to protect the broadcasting authorities' legal ownership.

At least as important as the training of teachers is the training of children in the use and appreciation of schools broadcasts in particular and the communications media in general. It is plainly desirable that children should know how to take advantage of material directed to them. But we also think it important that before they step out into a world where communications systems are so extensive and influential, they should be given a thorough grounding, not only in the technology of communications but in the appreciation and criticism of general programmes put out by the broadcasting services. Critical awareness might well be improved if communications were incorporated as a subject in every school curriculum. We should also advocate further research into childrens' attitudes to schools television, since there is some indication that children saturated by television at home may react against it at school or, familiar with colour television at home, regard material on black and white television as outdated or, habituated to the idea of television as entertainment, fail to realise its advantage as a medium for learning.

One of the few completely confident predictions we are prepared to make is that during the remainder of this century, education will be viewed as something which continues throughout life rather than as an activity confined to schools, universities, etc., that the popular demand for life-long education will increase, and that radio and television will prove to be major instruments for the satisfaction of this demand. We believe that the success of the Open University, despite pessimistic forecasts, is the beginning of an educational revolution. Currently, forty thousand students are enrolled on its books and pursuing courses leading to first degrees. The first successful candidates have already borne witness to the effectiveness of its tutorial system, to which radio and television courses are linked. Its operation has also revealed that there is a considerable audience of eavesdroppers listening to and viewing its programmes without seeking enrolment or intending to be examined, and that over-air broadcasting is at present, and for some years to come will remain, the most economical way of providing courses of instruction for students with no, or very varied, educational backgrounds, and drawn from a variety of professions and occupations. Currently there are also several thousand students enrolled for post-experience courses, that is, single courses rather than the full Open University degree. The present five-year agreement provides for 30 hours a week of broadcasting on each medium without specifying the timing of broadcasts. Currently there are 42 full- and half-time courses supported by 16½ hours of radio and 17½ hours of television per week. By 1975 there will be up to 75 full- and half-time courses supported by a maximum of 30 hours of radio and 30 hours of television per week. The long-term aim of the Open University is to have the equivalent of 110 full courses by 1981.

It is already clear that the BBC is strained to find radio and television time for the Open University courses. The problem is heightened since the Open University broadcasting must be at times when students can listen or view – in practice, the evening hours and at weekends. Until 1985, when a VHF television channel could become available, the only conceivable way of providing extra airtime is by allocating a substantial part of a radio channel and the fourth television channel to the Open University. This would blend in with the extra time required by Further Education and daytime hours for schools broadcasting, and still allow room for extra access television and regional or minority interests. The pressure for educational radio and television channels will be intensified if, as we would hope, the Open University proves to be a trail blazer for the Open College and the Open School. For the lesson of the Open University is that radio and television can help the adult whose schooling has been inadequate, or who has failed during his school years to take advantage of his opportunities, to equip himself later in life with a basic education or to move on to a further stage which under the traditional institutional system would have been difficult. Certainly the argument is based on the premise that raising standards of education, levelling up educational opportunities and spreading new methods and ideas is a task which broadcasting is peculiarly able to perform, and of such national importance that it is worth sacrificing other possible uses of the media, but for this we make no apology.

This statement leads on to consideration of Further Education, and special educational needs viewed as a whole. We have already stated our belief that educative programmes in good measure should be part of the programming on the general channels, and out of these general programmes there can, and often does, develop an appetite for systematic knowledge of an art, science or hobby. For such people and for all those who have a special interest are designed the BBC's Further Education series on radio and television, under the guidance of its Further Education Advisory Council, and the IBA's Adult Education programmes under its Adult Education Committee. These programmes cover a wide variety of vocational or recreational skills and learning, from dress-making and car-driving, and training courses for engineers and accountants, to series which help doctors and teachers keep abreast of new developments in their professions, and in-service training like the recent large-scale multi-media course on the raising of the school-leaving age. There are also many series on music, the arts, modern languages, the family and community, etc. The only limitation on Further Education is once again that of available time, and time available at the hours when it is most needed. It would, we believe, be a mistake to shift the bulk of present programmes onto an educational channel, but there are small minority interests or courses for advanced learners (in languages, for example) which could quite reasonably be placed on an educational channel without impoverishing the general services.

There are also many needs which are only slowly coming to light which the Further Education services cannot satisfy, or can supply only on a limited scale, which again might qualify for time on an educational channel or network. These include, for example, special radio courses for the blind and television courses for the deaf; courses for the illiterate and semi-illiterate, who are more numerous than is commonly supposed; for the mentally and physically handicapped; for immigrant groups who need special instruction in the local language, law and customs; vocational and professional re-training courses and courses for those made redundant by changes in the pattern of industry and commerce, or who otherwise have to make a fresh start in later life. The value of such courses cannot always be judged merely in terms of the numbers who follow them, for their effects may bring about economic and social benefits to the whole national community as well as to the individual. Here again we can see a good case for direct subvention in particular instances by Government, industry and social organisations which need not, indeed must not, threaten the independence of the broadcasting institutions. We would also draw attention to the theoretical possibilities of, at one end of the scale, programmes designed to increase international understanding and, at the other, for programmes tailored to local and regional requirements. For this, the IBA's regional companies seem especially well adapted. It would be possible, for example, for Tyne Tees to provide programmes assisting in the re-training of the very high numbers of unemployed in that region, or for those companies serving large rural areas to provide programmes for local farmers, This, indeed, would be possible at the present time by utilising, during school vacations, the hours normally given over to schools broadcasts, and we see no reason why the IBA should not provide some of the post-experience courses for the Open University since these are not funded by the Department of Education and Science. In conclusion, it should not be overlooked that there are thought to be substantial numbers of people in the country who would benefit from courses on parenthood and the basic knowledge required for running a home, supplementing the schools' own work in these matters, or for young adults who have only developed an interest once they are faced with problems in their own daily life. Also for the numbers of people who would like to take an initiative in local community activities but require basic knowledge on how to set about it.

All this, we recognise, amounts to considerable expansion of educative and educational broadcasting services. In the long term, it is possible that technical developments like cable television, and the establishment of cassette libraries, will take some of the pressure off the over-air services. But we think it likely, even if the pace of change accelerates more than we expect, that, for the next twenty years at least, educational services will have to be supplied mainly by the present broadcasting institutions, even if the system of co-ordination, administration and financing is regulated by a new agency. The long tradition of educational broadcasting has led to an accumulation of experience, skills and techniques, on which to build. The world of education today is alive with new ideas and new possibilities. Radio and television can be of enormous utility in helping these fresh developments to become known and to raise the educational standards of the whole population in the United Kingdom. We believe that the Government should do everything in its power to ensure that educators and broadcasters alike have all they need to share their respective skills and so create educative and educational broadcasting services which will match national needs during the final quarter of this century.

CONCLUSION

An inquiry into the subject of Broadcasting, which has so many ramifications and covers such a multitude of issues, is like trying to squash a live octopus into a small string shopping bag. We are well aware that our Report omits, or only fleetingly considers, many aspects of its subjects, but we hope at least to have created a perspective in which these can be calmly discussed and assessed before final decisions are made. At the end of our work we are more than ever convinced how important it is to provide the United Kingdom with the best possible communications services, which are the central nervous system of a modern social and political community. We have sometimes spoken idealistically (but not more so than many of those already engaged in broadcasting who have given us the benefit of their knowledge and advice), not in any romantic spirit or unaware that ideals continually recede, but because they set standards and must be pursued even if they are rarely achieved. We have throughout accepted that broadcasting cannot and should not impose tastes and choices on listeners and viewers. But we believe it can and should make available to them all that is best in the range of human interests and activities – sometimes to solace, sometimes to challenge – but always with a profound respect for truth, and a serious regard for the human dignity and individual variety of its audience;

awaken dormant capacities, play an important part in remedying society's defects, and celebrate life in all its diversity. With this in mind we have tried to strike a balance between national, local and individual needs, between the solid achievements of the past and future developments, between professionalism and the provision of a means of expression for all who have something to say. We hope that those who read it will feel we have fulfilled our intention of stimulating a more general public debate.

SUMMARY OF RECOMMENDATIONS

1. A national Centre for Broadcasting is needed, independent of the Government and the broadcasting institutions, but consulted on long-term policy by both.

2. The independence of the broadcasting services in carrying out the work for which they are responsible should be understood as part of the country's unwritten constitution.

3. The definition of the aims of broadcasting should include explicit reference to broadcasting as an instrument for encouraging participatory democracy.

4. There is an urgent need for more long-term, in-depth research into the social effects of broadcasting, and the coordination of existing research.

5. Further study and public debate, such as the proposed Centre envisages, is called for to determine whether a fourth channel is needed and, if so, how it should be allocated. A majority of the Commission would favour an educational channel with some allocation of airspace to access broadcasting, experimental programmes, minority and regional interests and independent productions. A minority would favour allocation to the IBA.*

* One member of the Commission, Sir Ronald Gould, wished the fourth channel to go to the I.B.A. without further delay.

6. At least one-third of peak viewing time should be allocated to educative and informative programmes.

7. The Ministry of Posts and Telecommunications should conduct a greater variety of experiments into cable systems to determine that best suited to the needs of the United Kingdom, before making any final decision. Whatever cable system or systems may be adopted, they should be confined to local community and regional programming and/or information services.

8. The IBA should explore further ways of exercising an influence over programme scheduling, offer the regional companies development grants for regional and experimental programmes, increase the proportion of time on the national network at present shared by the regional companies, and appoint regional officers to each company.

9. Further studies should be made of ways in which advertising time is regulated in foreign countries.

10. An agreed proportion of the levy on commercial television companies' profits should be earmarked for the improvement of broadcasting.

11. At least one-third of the members of the General Advisory Councils should be appointed independently of the broadcasting institutions.

12. The BBC should improve both its internal and external consultative procedures before making substantial changes in programme policy.

13. The BBC should be more open and less defensive in the conduct of its business, and make the findings of its research department more easily accessible to the public.

14. Increases in the licence fee must be regarded as the necessary price of a public service vital to the public interest and be sufficient to relieve the BBC of excessive financial anxiety. The licence fee could be complemented by grants in aid for particular services (e.g. the costs of certain educational services) without prejudice to the Corporation's independence.

15. A majority of the Commission is in favour of setting up a Complaints Review Board, independent of the BBC and IBA, solely to consider charges of inaccuracy and misrepresentation laid against the Corporation and the Authority, only after the Institutions have failed to satisfy the complainant, and without prejudice to their ordinary rights in law. A minority of the Commission is opposed to this proposal for reasons outlined in our Report.

16. The possibility of a new agency to oversee educational broadcasting in general, and administer an educational channel and radio network, should be considered.

17. Schools should be adequately supplied by local education authorities with audio-visual equipment, and as many teachers as possible be trained in its use.

18. We would suggest that some instruction in the use and appreciation of radio and television should be attempted in every school, and the communications media be adopted as a subject of study in the curriculum at secondary level.

INDEX

E